ANTHOLOGY

— for —

MUSIC IN THE BAROQUE

Western Music in Context: A Norton History

Walter Frisch SERIES EDITOR

Music in the Medieval West, by Margot Fassler

Music in the Renaissance, by Richard Freedman

Music in the Baroque, by Wendy Heller

Music in the Eighteenth Century, by John Rice

Music in the Nineteenth Century, by Walter Frisch

Music in the Twentieth and Twenty-First Centuries, by Joseph Auner

ANTHOLOGY
— for —
MUSIC IN THE BAROQUE

Wendy Heller

Princeton University

W. W. NORTON & COMPANY
NEW YORK • LONDON

W. W. Norton & Company has been independent since its founding in 1923, when William Warder Norton and Mary D. Herter Norton first published lectures delivered at the People's Institute, the adult education division of New York City's Cooper Union. The firm soon expanded its program beyond the Institute, publishing books by celebrated academics from America and abroad. By midcentury, the two major pillars of Norton's publishing program—trade books and college texts—were firmly established. In the 1950s, the Norton family transferred control of the company to its employees, and today—with a staff of four hundred and a comparable number of trade, college, and professional titles published each year—W. W. Norton & Company stands as the largest and oldest publishing house owned wholly by its employees.

Editor: Maribeth Payne
Associate Editor: Justin Hoffman
Assistant Editor: Ariella Foss
Developmental Editor: Harry Haskell
Manuscript Editor: Jodi Beder
Project Editor: Jack Borrebach
Editorial Assistant: Michael Fauver
Electronic Media Editor: Steve Hoge
Marketing Manager, Music: Amy Parkin
Production Manager: Ashley Horna
Photo Editor: Stephanie Romeo
Permissions Manager: Megan Jackson
Text Design: Jillian Burr
Composition: Jouve North America
Manufacturing: Quad/Graphics—Fairfield, PA

ISBN: 978-0-393-92020-8

W. W. Norton & Company, Inc., 500 Fifth Avenue, New York, NY 10110-0017
wwnorton.com

W. W. Norton & Company, Ltd., Castle House, 75/76 Wells Street, London W1T 3QT

1 2 3 4 5 6 7 8 9 0

CONTENTS

CONCORDANCE

This anthology is a companion to my book *Music in the Baroque*, which is part of the series Western Music in Context: A Norton History. The anthology includes scores and analytical commentary for excerpts from a broad range of compositions and can be used on its own or in conjunction with *Music in the Baroque*.

In selecting works for the anthology, I have endeavored to provide students, instructors, and music lovers with a combination of familiar and unfamiliar works that reflect some of the diversity and richness of music in this period. Thus, in addition to excerpts from such masterworks as Monteverdi's *L'Orfeo* and Lully's *Armide*, I include some less readily available selections, such as Telemann's *Ouverture burlesque di Don Quixotte*, and selections from Vivaldi's Concerto for Viola d'amore and Lute, RV 540; Purcell's *King Arthur*; and Rameau's *Platée*. Given the space constraints, I included only representative works by Bach and Handel; students and instructors are encouraged to explore the many works available online and in other anthologies.

The analytical commentaries are not meant to be exhaustive, but rather to provide a starting point for further discussions. My goal has been to underscore the distinctive features of the works, the special moments in the surface of the music that move, amuse, or even shock the listener. In texted works, I have paid particular attention to the relationship between music and poetry; my discussions focus on formal structure as relevant, exploring as well vocal and instrumental writing, rhythmic design, contrapuntal techniques, and the unpredictable ways in which tonal language functions during the period. As scholars still debate the best ways to describe tonality in the seventeenth century, I have endeavored to use language that will be clear to most students, avoiding anachronistic approaches and terminology whenever possible.

In addition to those selections taken from published editions, I have included a number of newly edited works. To ensure clarity and readability, the double and triple measures found in many of the early Italian sources have been regularized, and treble and bass clefs have been substituted without comment. The spellings of French and Italian reflect modern usage. Translations are mine unless otherwise indicated. I have presented excerpts from opera libretti in a form as close as possible to that in which the poets prepared them—including line breaks, punctuation, and spacing—but including the adjustments and additions made by composers.

A wide range of recording options gives students and instructors flexibility in listening to anthology selections. StudySpace, Norton's online resource for students, provides links to stream nearly every anthology selection from Naxos (accessible via an institutional or individual subscription), as well as links to purchase and download recordings from iTunes and Amazon.

I wish to thank John Burkhalter, Harry Haskell, Mark Kroll, Nicholas Lockey, and Saraswathi Shukla, all of whom read through the anthology and offered excellent advice; Jeffrey Kurtzman for his assistance with the Monteverdi Vespers; Brian Clark for his edition of the Telemann; and Luis Valencia for editing Monteverdi's *Lamento della ninfa* for our graduate seminar. I am especially grateful to Princeton University Libraries and Ben Primer for permission to use a facsimile of their copy of the Corelli sonata. At W. W. Norton I am particularly grateful for the careful copyediting and proofreading of Jodi Beder and Debbie Nichols. Jack Borrebach and Justin Hoffman have done brilliant work coordinating the anthology, grappling with the complex problem of permissions, and helping to assemble and set the scores.

Wendy Heller

ANTHOLOGY

— *for* —

MUSIC IN THE BAROQUE

CLAUDIO MONTEVERDI (1567–1643)

Fifth Book of Madrigals: *O Mirtillo*
Madrigal, published 1605

O Mirtillo, Mirtill'anima mia,	*O Myrtillus, Myrtillus, my soul,*
Se vedesti qui dentro	*If you could see inside*
Come sta il cor di questa	*how fares the heart of this girl*
Che chiami crudelissima Amarilli,	*that you call cruelest Amaryllis,*
So ben che tu di lei	*I know well that you, for her*
Quella pietà, che da lei chiedi, avresti.	*would have that pity which you demand from her.*
O anime in amor troppo infelici!	*O souls too unhappy in love!*
Che giova a te, cor mio, l'esser amato?	*What joy is it for you, my heart, to be loved?*
Che giova a me l'aver sì caro amante?	*What joy is it to me to have so beloved a lover?*
Perché, crudo destino,	*Why, cruel destiny,*
Ne disunisci tu, s'Amor ne stringe?	*do you part us, if Love binds us?*
E tu perché ne stringi,	*And why do you unite us,*
Se ne parte il destin, perfido Amore?	*if destiny is to part us, treacherous Love?*

Claudio Monteverdi opened his Fifth Book of Madrigals (1605) with settings of texts taken from Battista Guarini's popular tragicomedy *Il pastor fido* (The Faithful Shepherd), written for the Este court in Ferrara in the 1580s. From Act 1, he included Myrtillus's condemnation of Amaryllis's cruelty, "Cruda Amarilli," a text also set by a number of Monteverdi's contemporaries. This is followed by "O Mirtillo," from Act 3, scene 4 of the play, in which Amaryllis laments hiding her love from Myrtillus.

These two madrigals were to inspire their own controversy, independent of Guarini's work. In a famous dispute with Monteverdi, the theorist Giovanni Maria Artusi condemned "Cruda Amarilli" for its unprepared dissonances and "O Mirtillo" for its "improper" mixture of modes, dubbing the latter a "monster" made up of parts of various animals. While later commentators have been less harsh than Artusi, they too have been struck by oddities in the madrigal's tonal organization, even disagreeing about the madrigal's tonal center.

We have a hint of what might have concerned Artusi by comparing the opening and closing of the madrigal. While most madrigals begin and end on the same chord, "O Mirtillo" begins with a B♭ chord in the flat region (described by sixteenth- and seventeenth-century musicians as theorists as "soft" or *mollis*) and ends on a D-major sonority in the sharp or "hard" (*durus*) realm.

Artusi's "monster," however, makes a good deal of sense when we look more closely at the text. In the first part of the poem, Amaryllis imagines herself speaking to Myrtillus. First she declares her love for him ("O Myrtillus, my soul") in measures 1–5 with a pair of cadences on F and G respectively. She then expresses the impossible desire to have him see into her heart so he would know she is full of pity rather than cruelty. It is this conditional phrase—"if you could see"—that Monteverdi dramatizes with a somewhat meandering tonal scheme. One of the most poignant moments in the madrigal begins in measure 15 (line 4 of the poem) as Amaryllis contemplates the cruelty that Myrtillus has ascribed to her, "the most cruel Amaryllis." To mark this self-deprecating moment, Monteverdi slows the pace to half notes and shifts to a more imitative texture, while the stepwise descending lines initiate a series of suspensions culminating in an authentic cadence on G major (m. 29), decorated by the 2–3 suspension between alto and soprano in the previous bar. G minor is invoked only three measures later, as Amaryllis now contemplates the pity (pietà) she imagines Myrtillus might have for her, were he able to know her true feelings. By the time we land on the A-major sonority that marks the end of the poem's first part (m. 35), the listener might well claim to have the same trouble discerning the madrigal's tonal scheme that Myrtillus has had penetrating the secrets of his beloved's heart.

In the second half of the poem, as Amaryllis shifts her focus to the universal problems shared by all lovers separated by fate, the tonal organization is somewhat more stable. The first strong articulation of D major—and the only melismatic passage in the entire madrigal—occurs on the climactic utterance that begins the phrase "O souls too unhappy in love!" (mm. 35–36), which sends the soprano soaring into the upper register, leading to a plagal (IV–I) cadence on G. This section provides an excellent example of how artfully Monteverdi shifts between *durus* and *mollis* sonorities, sometimes using B♮ and other times B♭, in response to the text and the principles of the *seconda prattica*. Beginning in measure 42, as the protagonist contemplates the joys of being loved and loving, Monteverdi uses B♮ and sonorities on the sharp side of the tonal spectrum; the homophonic passage in measures 46–51 culminates finally in the first definitive D-major cadence on the word "amante" (lover) more than two-thirds of the way through the madrigal. This happiness is mere illusion, and Monteverdi immediately reintroduces the B♭ in the soprano in measures 51–52 on the word "crudo" (cruel). However, in the next measure, as Amaryllis decides that it is fate (rather than her own harshness) that separates her from her Myrtillus, the B♭ vanishes, never to return. Myrtillus may not be able to see into the heart of Amaryllis, but Monteverdi's interpretation of the poem allows us to understand not only the depth of her despair but the pain experienced by every lover whose happiness is thwarted by destiny.

Subtle changes in meaning and affect are achieved not only through tonal means and melodic design, but also through alterations in scoring and texture. It is significant, for example, that the only time other than the beginning and ending in which Monteverdi uses all five voices is in the passage in measures 23–29 during which the name of the "most cruel Amaryllis" is invoked. Otherwise, Monteverdi omits one or another voice, not only shifting from imitative to homophonic textures, but altering the scoring, even when a given line of text is repeated and transposed. Compare, for instance, the setting of lines 2–3 of the poem (beginning in the second half of m. 5) with its repetition starting on beat 2 of measure 10. Monteverdi reduces the scoring from four voices to three, placing each phrase on a different pitch level: the line beginning "Se vedesti qui dentro" is transposed down a fifth in measures 10–12, while the next phrase ("Come sta il cor di questa") is transposed down a fourth (mm. 12–14). What might have been a simple repetition of both music and text is transformed and intensified with dramatic contrasts of texture, scoring, and tonality that characterize Monteverdi's masterful approach to text setting.

2

GIULIO CACCINI (1551–1618)

Le nuove musiche: Dovrò dunque morire
Solo song, published 1602

From Giulio Caccini, *Le nuove musiche*, ed. H. Wiley Hitchcock, Recent Researches in the Music of the Baroque Era, vol. 9. Middleton, WI: A-R Editions, Inc., 2009. Used with permission. All rights reserved.

voi: "Mo- ro, mia vi- ta." O_____ mi-

[handwritten: say to you, "I die, my life."]

-se- ria in- au- di- ta, non po- ter dir a

voi: mo- ro, mia vi- ta, non_____ po- ter dir a voi: "Mo-

- ro, mia vi- ta, mo- ro,_____ mia_____

vi- - ta."_____

Dovrò dunque morire,	*Must I thus die*
pria che di nuovo io miri	*before I see you again,*
voi, bramata cagion de' miei martiri?	*you, desired cause of my suffering?*
Mio perduto tesoro,	*My lost treasure,*
non potrò dirvi, pria ch'io mora: "Io moro?"	*could I not say to you, before I die: "I die"?*
O miseria inaudita,	*O unheard misery,*
non poter dir a voi: "Moro, mia vita."	*not being able to say to you: "I die, my life."*

Giulio Caccini included "Dovrò dunque morire" in his landmark 1602 publication *Le nuove musiche* (The New Musical Works). Yet, as we learn from the preface to that volume, this elegant love song was actually composed in the 1580s, while Caccini was associated with the Florentine Camerata led by Count Giovanni de' Bardi. It must have enjoyed considerable popularity, as it can be found in slightly different versions in several manuscripts, including two that transmit the song with lute tablature.

Like the other works in *Le nuove musiche*, "Dovrò dunque morire" does not include a fully written out accompaniment, but only a basso continuo: a bass line suggesting chords that can be realized by a lute or harpsichord, supported, if desired, by a bowed bass instrument. By this means, Caccini created a type of song "by which anyone could almost speak in music, using . . . a certain noble *sprezzatura* [calculated negligence] in the melody, passing sometimes over some discords while sustaining the pitch of the bass note . . . and with the middle lines played by the instrument to express some *affetto*" (SR 100:608; 4/ 20:100). This flexible approach enabled singers to shape the vocal line according to the dictates of the text, ideally following the instructions for ornamentation that Caccini included in the preface. The editor of the modern edition reproduced here includes parenthetical suggestions as to which ornaments Caccini might have recommended and where he might have placed them. The cadence in measure 8 would likely be ornamented with a *t[rillo]* (not a modern trill but increasingly rapid repetitions of a single note), whereas in measure 20 Caccini might have encouraged the singer to use an *escl[amazione]* (which he described as a gradual relaxing of the voice on a held note, resulting in a change in intensity). The lutenist or harpsichordist also had the freedom to use more or less intricate counterpoint or play cadential chords with major rather than minor sonorities when not otherwise marked.

The brief poem by Ottavio Rinuccini, another member of Bardi's circle, features the combination of 7- and 11-syllable lines that was popular in Italian poetry of the period. At the outset the poet's complaint of unrequited love seems conventional enough: "Must I thus die before I see you again?" However, by the fifth line it becomes apparent that "death" refers not only to loss of life, but also to the poet's sexual fulfillment: he fears that he won't have the opportunity to exclaim "I die" in the arms of his lover before his own death. The final two lines of the poem reiterate the same sentiments, with subtle changes. The poet's misery is as silent, or "inaudita" (unheard), as is his expression of passion. The final reference to the beloved as "mia vita" (my life) underscores the antithesis between life and death, both real and metaphorical. The multiple layers of antithesis are reinforced by the contrasting vowels, such as the emphasis on the "o" sound, particularly apparent in the various forms of the word "morire" (to die), as compared with the "i" of "vita" (life).

Caccini's setting captures all of these subtleties. Of particular note is the heightened intensity beginning at line 5 (m. 23) as the erotic implications of the poet's desire become explicit. In fact, Caccini sets the poem asymmetrically: the first five lines of the poem comprise only 18 of the song's 47 measures. Of the 29 measures that Caccini used to set the final two lines, a full 14 are devoted to the final statement of the poem's last line, prolonged by word repetitions and an elaborate melisma on "vita" (m. 44.)

The tonal language highlights this division of the song into two unequal parts. Caccini uses the juxtaposition of Bb and B♮ as a sonic equivalent of the antithesis between the two types of death. The unambiguous sense of G minor in the opening is disturbed by the introduction of B♮s, first in the bass in measure 13, then in the melody in measure 15, and still more blatantly in such instances as the exclamation of "O" in measures 19 and 29. These G-major sonorities do not necessarily convey a more cheerful affect. Rather, in contrast with the flat (mollis) G-minor sonorities, the sharp (durus) G major expresses something of the lover's erotic intensity. As we saw with "O Mirtillo" (see Anthology 1), the juxtaposition of sharp and flat sonorities was a valuable device for expressing sudden emotional shifts.

The sense of spontaneity—the sprezzatura that Caccini so prized—is somewhat contrived. Although there is relatively little repetition of music over the course of the song (a notable exception being the settings of "non poter dir a voi" in mm. 23–25 and 36–38), Caccini concentrates on a few motivic ideas. The opening phrase, for instance, sets up a sense of longing with the stepwise ascent from the Bb to the sustained D on the word "dunque," while also providing an opportunity for ornamentation. The poet's yearning is represented in the constant effort to return to the D and sustain it on various iterations of the word "moro" (mm. 16–17, 25–26, and 38–39). The melisma on "inaudita" (m. 31) is echoed on "vita" (m. 44), underscoring the rhyme. The result is a sophisticated and subtle expression of erotic desire that surely accounts for the song's popularity in the late sixteenth and early seventeenth centuries.

3

aabbcc

JOHN DOWLAND (1563–1626)

Second Booke of Songs or Ayres: Flow, my tears
Solo song, published 1600

Lament:
A-G-F-E

VOICE

Flow, my tears, fall / from your springs! Ex - iled / for ev- er, let me mourn; Where
Down, vain lights, shine / you no more! No nights are dark e-nough for those That

LUTE

1. Use of Rit.
2. Trills on repeat

night's black / bird her sad in - fa-my sings, There / let me live for -
in de - spair their lost for - tunes de - plore. Light / doth but shame dis -

From John Dowland, *Second Book of Songs* (1600), ed. Edmund H. Fallows, rev. ed. Thurston Dart, The English Lute Songs, series 1, vols. 5–6 (London: Stainer and Bell, 1969), 4–6. © 1922, 1969 Stainer & Bell Ltd. Reproduced by permission.

Flow, my tears, fall from your springs!
Exiled forever, let me mourn;
Where night's black bird her sad infamy sings,
There let me live forlorn.

Down vain lights, shine you no more!
No nights are dark enough for those
That in despair their lost fortunes deplore.
Light doth but shame disclose.

Never may my woes be relieved,
Since pity is fled;
And tears and sighs and groans my weary days
Of all joys have deprived.

From the highest spire of contentment
My fortune is thrown;
And fear and grief and pain for my deserts
Are my hopes, since hope is gone.

Hark! you shadows that in darkness dwell,
Learn to contemn light.
Happy, happy they that in hell
Feel not the world's despite.

⚜

"Flow, my tears" was first published in John Dowland's *Second Booke of Songs or Ayres of 2, 4, and 5 parts* (1600). Dowland was serving King Christian IV of Denmark, having left England some six years previously after being passed over for the appointment he desired in Queen Elizabeth's court.

The song has a complex history, as both a vocal and instrumental composition. The first published version included a second vocal part for bass, placed on the side of the printed page where it could easily be read by an additional singer (see Fig. 2.3 in *Music in the Baroque*). The version for solo voice presented here is heard more frequently. However, Dowland had written at least one earlier version of the song as a pavan (a slow, dignified dance in duple meter) for solo lute in the 1590s. The tune also became the basis for his cycle of pieces entitled *Lachrimae, or Seaven Teares* (1604), and was used for sets of variations by colleagues in both England and Europe, including William Byrd, Thomas Morley, and Jan Pieterszoon Sweelinck. While it is impossible to ascertain which was the "original" version of the music, it seems likely that the poem—probably written by Dowland himself—was fitted after the initial composition of the melody; this would explain both its close rapport with the melody and its somewhat irregular meter. The unrelentingly mournful affect is also unusual in this repertory. The poet does not ask for respite from his grief; rather, he pleads that his misery continue unabated.

The song is divided into three sections of unequal lengths, each of which is repeated; the musical form is thus **AABBCC**. The first and second sections present strophes 1–2 and 3–4, respectively, while in the third section the fifth strophe is repeated. Although the sections are somewhat related motivically, each has a distinctive rhythmic and melodic profile and employs a different tonal strategy. Section 1 is primarily in A minor, concluding with a major-mode cadence. Section 2 (mm. 8–15) begins in C but soon returns to A minor, reaching an E-major sonority via a Phrygian cadence (motivating a return to A minor). Section 3 begins on an E-major chord (m. 16) and returns to A minor, albeit with a Picardy third at the conclusion.

The mournful tone is established in measure 1 by Dowland's signature "tear motive"—a stepwise descending tetrachord from A to E. This is answered in the same measure by another statement of the four-note motive between C and G♯, creating a poignant cross-relation with the G♮ heard earlier in the measure. This descending fourth dominates the entire song. For instance, it is presented as a skip on the word "exiled" (m. 2). The diminished fourth between C and G♯ is reiterated three times in measures 4–6, first by means of inter-locking descending thirds ("night's black bird her"), then stepwise ("infamy sings"), and finally in an ornamented stepwise version, before resolving on a major cadence thanks to a Picardy third that briefly mitigates the poet's sorrow ("there let me live forlorn").

In the second section, the transposition of the descending-fourth motive to a C-major environment (with G♮ rather than G♯) provides a hint of optimism (m. 8) that is contradicted by the poem, where relief (strophe 3) and content-ment (strophe 4) are presented as unattainable. This sense of gloom is sup-ported musically in measures 9–10 with the return to A minor. There is a brief sense of renewed energy beginning in measure 11 as the sequence of ascending thirds, broken up by rests and imitated by the lute, conveys the poet's breath-less anticipation. Depression returns, however, as C major gives way to minor sonorities. The ornamented Phrygian cadence on E (mm. 14–15) reiterates the tear motive. This section transitions seamlessly to the next through the rep-etition of the G♯ (and accompanying E-major sonority). As the melody traces the space between G♯ and C in longer note values (mm. 16–18), first ascending stepwise and then descending by step, lethargy sets in. This leads to the high-est pitch and the climax of the song (m. 19), a repetition of "happy" on a pair of interlocking descending fourths.

The prominence of the word "happy" in the context of the poet's misery raises an interesting question. Is this an instance in which Dowland, hav-ing written the poem after the music, fails to match tone and word? Or should we hear it instead as a cry of desperation, revealing the poet's inner yearning for release? Whatever optimism this might inspire about the poet's capacity to experience pleasure disappears as the melodic line falls to G$\sharp$ on the word "hell" in measure 20, followed by a final iteration of the descending diminished fourth and its resolution. The expressivity throughout is heightened by contrapuntal interweavings of the melody with the lute's inner voices, resulting in affecting dissonances and cross-relations.

"Flow, my tears" reflects the early modern fascination (particularly pronounced in England) with melancholy, regarded as a disease caused by an excess of black bile, one of the four humors that were the basis of medicine in this period. As Dowland's contemporary Richard Burton observed in his *Anatomy of Melancholy* (1621): "Many men are melancholy by hearing music, but it is a pleasing melancholy that it causeth; and therefore, to such as are discontent, in woe, fear, sorrow, or dejected, it is a most present remedy; it expels cares, alters their grieved minds, and easeth in an instant."

4

CLAUDIO MONTEVERDI (1567–1643)

L'Orfeo, Act 2: *Tu se' morta* and *Ahi, caso acerbo*
Opera, 1607

Recitative: *Tu se' morta*

Choral madrigal: *Ahi, caso acerbo*

5

se; ahi, cie - lo a - va - ro! Non si fi-di uom mor - ta - le
se; ahi, cie - lo a - va - ro! Non si fi - di uom mor - ta - le
se; ahi, cie - lo a - va - ro! Non si fi - di uom mor - ta - le
se; ahi, cie - lo a - va - ro! Non si fi - di uom mor - ta - le di ben case; ahi, cie - lo a - va - ro! Non si fi - di uom mor - ta - le

9

di ben ca-du - co e fra-le, che to-sto fug-ge, e spes - so
di ben ca-du - co e fra-le, che to-sto fug-ge, che to-sto fug-ge, e spes - so
di ben ca-du-co e fra - le, che to-sto fug-ge, che to-sto fug-ge, e spes - so
du - co e fra-le, che to-sto fug-ge, che to-sto fug-ge, e spes - so a gran-sa
di ben ca-du - co e fra - le, che to-sto fug-ge, e spes - so

13

a gran sa-li - ta a gran sa-li - ta il pre-ci - pi-zio è pres - so.
a gran sa-li - ta a gran sa-li - ta il pre-ci-pi - zio è pres - so.
a gran sa-li - ta a gran sa-li - ta il pre-ci-pi - zio è pres - so.
ti - ca a gran sa-li - ta il pre-ci - pi - zio è pres - so.
a gran sa-li - ta a gran sa-li - ta il pre-ci-pi - zio è pres - so.

ORPHEUS

Tu se' morta, mia vita, ed io respiro?	*You are dead, my life, and I breathe?*
Tu se' da me partita	*You have, left me,*
per mai più non tornare, ed io rimango?	*never to return, and I breathe?*
No, che se i versi alcuna cosa ponno	*No, if verses can do anything,*
n'andrò sicuro a più profondi abissi,	*I will surely go to the deepest abyss*
e, intenerito il cor del Re del'ombre,	*and charm the heart of the king of the shadows*
meco trarrotti a riveder le stelle:	*and bring you back with me to see the stars:*
O se ciò negherammi empio destino,	*Oh, if evil destiny denies me this,*
rimarrò teco in compagnia di morte.	*I will remain with you in the company of death.*
Addio, terra; addio, cielo e sole; addio.	*Farewell, earth; farewell, heavens and sun; farewell.*

CHORUS

Ahi, caso acerbo; ahi, fato empio e crudele;	*Ah, bitter mischance; ah, wicked, cruel fate;*
ahi, stelle ingiuriose; ahi, ciel avaro!	*Ah, hurtful stars; ah, envious heaven!*
Non si fidi uom mortale	*Let no mortal man trust*
di ben caduco e frale,	*happiness that is passing and frail,*
che tosto fugge, e spesso	*that soon flies away and oft*
a gran salita il precipizio è presso.	*at the precipice is near a great height.*

When Claudio Monteverdi and Alessandro Striggio first presented *L'Orfeo* (Orpheus) at a meeting of the Mantuan Accademia degli Invaghiti (Academy of the Lovestruck) on February 24, 1607, they could scarcely have imagined both the fame the work would achieve and the significance that its hero would have in the history of opera. Theirs was not the first stage work based on Ovid's tale of Orpheus and Eurydice. Not only did Striggio and Monteverdi set out to emulate the Florentine *Euridice* (1600), with settings by both Jacopo Peri and Ottavio Rinuccini, they also may have been paying homage to Angelo Poliziano's popular humanist drama on the subject, produced in Mantua in the late fifteenth century.

In their hands, however, Orpheus became the prototype of the ideal operatic hero. His trip to Hades not only provided an opportunity for scenic display, but also had a moral component: it invoked Christian ideas about the underworld popularized in the late Middle Ages by Dante, reminding viewers that Orpheus, like Christ, is in a sense resurrected. Moreover, since the legendary singer and lyre player uses the power of music to persuade Pluto to release his beloved Eurydice from death, the tale provides a natural opportunity for singing—what is sometimes referred to as "phenomenal music," whereby a character on stage plays, sings, or listens to actual music. Thus, numerous later Orpheus operas, including settings by Luigi Rossi (1647), Marc-Antoine Charpentier (ca. 1685), Georg Philipp Telemann (1722), Franz Joseph Haydn (1791), Jacques Offenbach (1858), and Philip Glass (1993), feature scenes in which Orpheus laments the loss of his wife and demonstrates his musical skill in the underworld.

In Monteverdi's opera, Orpheus's first lament comes at the climax of Act 2. Rejoicing in the aftermath of his marriage, Orpheus is interrupted as the messenger arrives with the harsh news of his wife's death from a serpent ("Ahi, caso acerbo"), the bitterness of which is heightened by Monteverdi's dissonant setting. After hearing the messenger's description of Eurydice's tragic demise, Orpheus laments her loss with "Tu se' morta." The first part of the recitative presents the grieving Orpheus in an almost catatonic state, as he grapples with the fact that he lives and breathes while Eurydice lies dead. The unexpected rests that break the first line of text into melodic fragments evoke Orpheus's irregular breathing and apparent inertia. The dissonances and cross-relations not only reflect his sorrow but also underscore the antithesis between death and life that is the heart of the matter. This effect is created by the sudden clash between the F♯ in the vocal line and the G in the bass in measure 2, and the cross-relation between G♯ and G♮ in measure 4. The juxtaposition of *mollis* (flat) and *durus* (sharp) sonorities also mirrors Orpheus's conflicted state: he begins on a G-minor sonority, moves to E major to color the phrase "mia vita" (my life) by introducing a B♮ in measure 3, and then slips back into G minor in the next measure.

Monteverdi's subtle alterations to Striggio's poetry shape and intensify Orpheus's monologue. Monteverdi expands Striggio's "tu se', tu se' pur ita" (you are, you are really gone) in line 2 to "tu se', tu se' da me partita" (you have, *you have* left me), which not only heightens the intensity, but creates an echo of the opening of the recitative that Monteverdi exploits musically.

As Orpheus's despair turns into determination, so too Monteverdi alters his mode of expression. In measure 8, the B♭ disappears from the key signature; the bass moves decisively, often by fifth, and the melodic contour becomes more lyrical. Monteverdi uses text painting to illustrate the journey to Hades that Orpheus proposes to make and underscore the poetic contrasts. For instance, the description of the "più profondi abissi" (deepest abyss) sends the melody down to a low C; Orpheus's vision of Eurydice returning to see the stars (a striking quote from Dante) is represented by his use of the upper register; and the words "di morte" (of death) are ominously colored with an E♭. His final farewell is most dramatic, with its chromatic ascent through B♭ and B♮ to high D, followed by an abrupt downward plunge. The chorus then joins in their own acknowledgment of the tragedy with a less dissonant version of the messenger's cry "Ahi, caso acerbo," concluding the scene in contrasting flat sonorities with a sober reflection on the fleeting nature of happiness.

CLAUDIO MONTEVERDI (1567–1643)

Madrigali guerrieri et amorosi: Lamento della ninfa
Madrigal (with continuo), published 1638

Non avea Febo ancora

Trampling

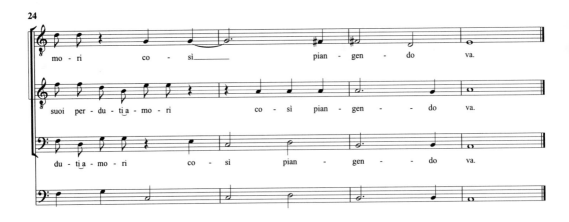

Lamento della ninfa

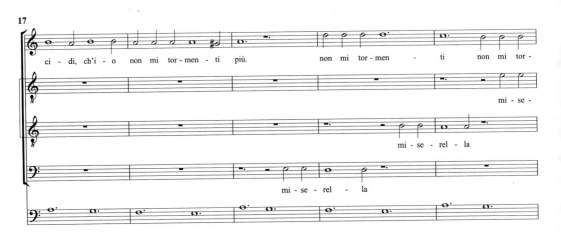

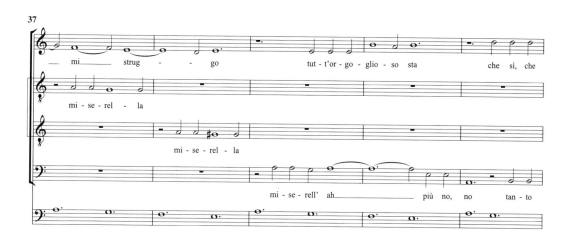

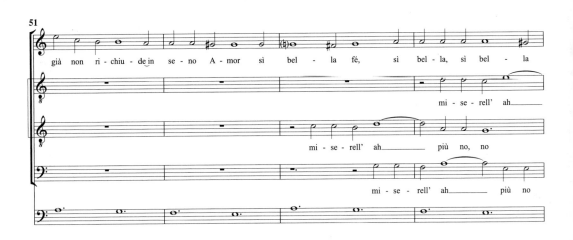

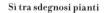

Sì tra sdegnosi pianti

PART 1: MADRIGAL FOR THREE MALE VOICES

Non avea Febo ancora	*Phoebus had not yet*
recato al mondo il dì,	*brought to daylight the world*
ch'una donzella fuora	*when a damsel*
del proprio albergo uscì.	*came out of her dwelling.*
Sul pallidetto volto	*On her pale face*
scorgeasi il suo dolor,	*her suffering was apparent,*
spesso gli venia sciolto	*and often she let escape*
un gran sospir dal cor.	*a great sigh from her heart.*
Sì calpestando fiori,	*Thus trampling flowers,*
errava, or qua or là,	*she wandered here and there,*
i suoi perduti amori	*[over] her lost loves,*
così piangendo va.	*thus crying.*

PART 2: LAMENT FOR SOPRANO AND THREE MALE VOICES

"Amor, dicea," il ciel	*"Love," she said, stopping*
mirando il pie fermò,	*to look at the heavens,*
"dove, dov'è la fé	*"where, where is the faith*
che'l traditor giurò?"	*that the traitor swore to me?"*
Miserell' ah più no, no	Miserable girl, alas, no longer
tanto gel soffrir non può.	can she suffer such scorn.
"Fa che ritorni il mio	*"Let my love return to me*
amor com'ei pur fu,	*as he was,*
o tu m'ancidi, ch'io	*or else kill me, so that I*
non mi tormenti più."	*will no longer torment myself."*
Miserell' ah più no, no	Miserable girl, alas, no longer
tanto gel soffrir non può.	can she suffer such scorn.

"Non vo' più ch'ei sospiri
se non lontan da me
no, no ch'ei suoi martiri
più non dirammi a fé."
Miserell' ah più no, no
tanto gel soffrir non può.

"Perché di lui mi struggo
tutt'orgoglioso sta
che sì, che sì se'l fuggo
ancor mi pregherà?"
Miserell' ah più no, no
tanto gel soffrir non può.

"Se ciglio ha più sereno
colei, ch'el mio non è,
già non richiude in seno
Amor sì bella fé."
Miserell' ah più no, no
tanto gel soffrir non può.

"Né mai sì dolci baci
da quella bocca avrà,
né più soavi—ah taci,
taci che troppo il sa."
Miserell' ah più no, no
tanto gel soffrir non può.

"I don't want him to sigh
unless he is far away from me
no, no, he will no longer
tell me of his sufferings, I swear."
Miserable girl, alas, no longer
can she suffer such scorn.

"Because I suffer for him,
he is full of pride.
Yet, if I were to flee from him,
would he still want me?"
Miserable girl, alas, no longer
can she suffer such scorn.

"If she [the other woman] has a more serene
brow than mine,
She does not hold in her breast,
Oh Love, faithfulness as beautiful as mine."
Miserable girl, alas, no longer
can she suffer such scorn.

"Never will he have such sweet kisses,
from that mouth,
or sweeter—ah, be silent,
be silent, that he knows [it] all too well."
Miserable girl, alas, no longer
can she suffer such scorn.

PART 3: MADRIGAL FOR THREE MALE VOICES

Sì tra sdegnosi pianti
spargea le voci al ciel,
così ne' cori amanti,
mesce Amor fiamma e gel.

So among the scornful weeping
she scattered her words to the sky,
thus in lovers' hearts
Love mixes flame and ice.

Claudio Monteverdi published the *Lamento della ninfa* (Lament of the Nymph) in 1638 in his eighth book of madrigals, titled *Madrigali guerrieri et amorosi* (Warlike and Loving Madrigals) and dedicated to the Habsburg emperor Ferdinand III. In dividing the book into songs of war and songs of love, Monteverdi exploited the dramatic potential of contrasting bellicose and amorous modes of expression. These were not as incompatible as one might imagine: poets from ancient to early modern times, such as Ovid and Petrarch, used war as a metaphor to describe the sufferings of the lover and the battle that must be pursued to conquer the reluctant maiden.

One of the "madrigali amorosi," the *Lamento della ninfa* depicts an abandoned nameless nymph (referred to only as "miserella," or miserable girl) who wanders about at dawn bemoaning the loss of her lover. The poem by Ottavio Rinuccini is typically referred to as a *canzonetta*. In its original form (before Monteverdi set it to music), each of the ten stanzas included four lines plus a two-line refrain (printed in italics above), yielding the rhyme scheme *ababcc*.

While most composers set canzonettas as strophic songs, Monteverdi here does something entirely novel. He exploits the inherent drama of the situation by creating a three-part scene—a genuine staged drama, which he called the *genere rappresentativo* (dramatic genre). The strophes in which the girl is described (stanzas 1–3 and 10) are set homophonically ("Non avea Febo ancora" and "Sì tra sdegnosi pianti") and sung by two tenors and a bass, using particularly vivid text painting: note the dissonance on the word "suo" (her) in measure 11 (an F♮, G♯, and E sounding together), preparing us for "dolor" (suffering); the illustration of the sighs in measures 14–17; and the stomping on the flowers in measures 18–23.

Monteverdi, with his usual penchant for "recomposing" the poetry he set, omits the refrain ("Miserella," etc.) in the three strophes sung by the male trio. However, he puts it to good use in the settings of strophes 4–9, the nymph's actual lament. Here all semblance of the canzonetta disappears as Monteverdi places her impassioned aria over a descending tetrachord ostinato consisting of the pitches A–G–F–E. Her expressions of grief and sorrow—her dismay at her lover's infidelity, her fantasies about the woman who has replaced her, and her convictions that her lover will never enjoy sweeter kisses or greater fidelity—are accompanied and punctuated by the interjections of three male witnesses, who sing portions of the two-line refrain throughout.

Unlike Orpheus's lament "Tu se' morta" (see Anthology 4), in which the realization of the continuo line followed and emphasized the mood changes in the text, the nymph's sorrow and obsession are represented by the rigid, almost hypnotic repetition of the pitches and rhythms of the descending tetrachord in a triple meter, rarely associated with lamentation. Against the constancy of the ground bass, the fragmenting of the melodic line (as in the repetitions of "Amor" in mm. 3–7) or its expansion (as in the long phrase in mm. 13–19) allows Monteverdi to capture minute changes in her emotional state. Moreover, the fact that the relationship of the vocal lines to this bass pattern is constantly changing allows for unexpected dissonances and cross-relations. Consider, for instance, the clash between the G♯ and A in measure 15 and between the G♮ and A in measure 31. Monteverdi also uses the vocal parts to follow or contradict the rhythm of the bass line, as in the syncopated passage in measures 35–38, where the nymph's vocal line, contesting the dominance of the bass, boldly descends by step to the low E with emphatic syncopations.

Textural interest is further enhanced by Monteverdi's varied treatment of the male trio. In some instances the tenors and bass function as a single unit responding homophonically to the nymph (most strikingly in the climactic dissonant cry in mm. 33–34). At other time, as in measures 42–44, one of the male voices intertwines with the nymph's for a brief duet laden with suspensions, alluding to the sensual pleasures that the nymph has lost but regretfully remembers all too well. The nymph's unhappiness is not communicated directly to the listener, but filtered through the gaze of the male onlookers, whose viewpoint frames what we see of her response.

We can learn something about Monteverdi's conception of this work from instructions he provided in the edition. The parts for the three men who sing the first and final sections, he indicates, are placed separately in part books, because "they sing at the tempo of the hand," that is, in a regular rhythm. However, in the central section the parts for the male singers are included in the score of the lament itself, since they sing "at the tempo of the affect of the soul, and not that of the hand," with greater rhythmic flexibility according to the passions of the text. In this way, the nymph and the men who accompany her are free to alter the tempo according to the dictates of the passions she is describing.

6

GIROLAMO FRESCOBALDI (1583–1643)

Toccate e partite d'intavolatura di cimbalo,
Book 1: Toccata No. 2
Keyboard toccata, published 1615

This G-minor toccata appears in Book 1 of Frescobaldi's *Toccate e partite d'intavolatura di cimbalo* (Toccatas and Partitas Scored for Harpsichord), first published in 1615 and dedicated to Ferdinando Gonzaga, duke of Mantua. The term *toccata*, derived from the Italian verb *toccare* "to touch," is one of many genre names used for keyboard pieces in the *stylus phantasticus*, or fantastic style, in which the keyboard player (or other instrumentalist) uses a quasi-improvisational style to create the impression that the piece is being made up on the spot. Characteristics of the style include rhythmic freedom and sudden changes in texture, affect, or register, along with flashes of virtuosity or demonstrations of contrapuntal skill. The fantastic style was an important feature of instrumental music throughout the Baroque and can be found to some degree in Castello's Sonata No. 2 (Anthology 7), the opening movement of Froberger's Suite in C Major (see Anthology 8), and some of the variations in Biber's *Crucifixion* Sonata (see Anthology 22). The fantastic style also exemplifies the dramatic and unconventional use of dissonance that we have seen in Monteverdi's vocal music (see Anthology 4 and 5).

Frescobaldi's collection proved so popular that a second edition was published in 1616, this time with an extensive preface in which Frescobaldi instructs players in detail about the correct way of performing the music, citing vocal music as his model. The "manner of playing," he observes, "should not remain subject to a beat," but should be similar "to modern madrigals," in which the beat is taken "now slowly, now rapidly, and even suspended in the air, according to the meaning of the words." He instructs keyboardists that the opening chords should be adagio and arpeggiated, and that the sections of the toccatas should be differentiated from one another according to their affects. Frescobaldi also tells players that they can conclude the piece at the close of any section without doing violence to the overall conception of the work. Frescobaldi likely used this same approach for his organ works, since the music often had to be coordinated to accompany a given liturgical event.

The Toccata No. 2 in G minor provides a good example of the fantastic style. The opening chords would have been arpeggiated and performed freely and slowly, likely taking up far more time than the notated rhythm. Measures 2–5 feature written-out ornaments and short melodic fragments that are passed from one voice to another; however, Frescobaldi soon abandons this contrapuntal texture in favor of virtuosic scalar passages, first for the right hand, then the left, and finally with the two combined (mm. 6–8). This improvisatory feeling, however, belies Frescobaldi's careful planning. In measure 9, for instance, Frescobaldi places the melodic gesture from the opening of the toccata (D–E♭–C) in the bass. This motive is then imitated in an ornamented fashion in the soprano, and is heard in sequential fashion in the other voices until the end of measure 11, when the sixteenth-note passagework once again takes command.

Indeed, a characteristic of the fantastic style is the relative ease with which the music moves from one to another idea or set of ideas in the various subsections delineated by the cadences. At the end of measure 13, for instance, Frescobaldi comes to a halt on a half cadence on A major, while measure 14 begins with a lively new set of ideas: concentrating in the middle register, Frescobaldi activates the alto and tenor voices, introducing a dotted motive that gets passed from voice to voice in measures 15–19. An unexpected burst of passagework, first in the right hand and then in the left, brings us to another moment of repose in measure 22—a single measure of sustained chords, with a striking dissonance (the B in the bass against the A in the treble) on beat 3, which resolves on the next beat. This transitions smoothly into a long section dominated by a melodic figure in Lombard rhythm (short-long) that culminates in what is essentially a written-out trill in the alto and tenor voices a third apart over an A-major chord (m. 27), preparing for the cadence on a first-inversion D-major chord in the following measure. This is also the beginning of a new section, in which the left hand takes over much of the passagework.

The cadence on D major in measure 33, marking the end of another section, does not return us to the home key; however, it is sufficiently definitive that Frescobaldi would have been quite content for the player to stop there, if necessary, to fit the requirements of the liturgy. Nonetheless, by measure 40 he has brought us securely back to G minor with a burst of virtuosity in the left hand and just a taste of C minor before the final measures, as the right and left hands join for a cadential flourish, leading to an arrival on G major with a Picardy third.

7 DARIO CASTELLO (FL. FIRST HALF OF 17TH CENTURY)

Sonate concertate in stil moderno,
Book 2: Sonata No. 2
Sonata for treble instrument and continuo, published 1629

From Dario Castello, *Sonate concertate: libro secondo* / Dario Castello; herausgegeben von Rudolf Hofstötter & Ingomar Rainer. © Copyright 1998 by Hochschule fuer Musik und Darstellende Kunst, University of Music and Performing Arts Vienna. Reprinted by permission.

Very little is known about the life of Dario Castello other than the brief details that can be gleaned from the title pages of his publications. In the early 1600s he was employed as a cornettist at St. Mark's Basilica in Venice, where he also led a wind ensemble. His fame rests largely upon his two volumes of *Sonate concertate in stil moderno* (Concerted Sonatas in Modern Style) for one or more instruments and continuo. Volume 1, published in 1621, was the first instrumental collection to use the word "sonata" in the title and to declare itself so boldly to be in the modern style.

Sonata, from the Italian verb "suonare" (to play), was used throughout the Baroque to refer to a variety of instrumental compositions, often for one or more instruments with continuo and usually divided into multiple movements or sections. Our anthology includes sonatas for violin and continuo by Arcangelo Corelli (see Anthology 17) and Heinrich Ignaz Franz Biber (see Anthology 22). Castello, no doubt aware that he was a pioneer, reassured his players in the preface that even though his sonatas "appear difficult at first sight, one should not lack confidence to play them more than once, because this will serve as practice, and after time they will be rendered more easily because no thing is difficult for the person who delights in it."

The Sonata No. 2 for violin (or cornetto) and continuo from Castello's second volume (1629) demonstrates how the "modern style" applied to a composition for solo treble instrument and continuo. Castello's sonatas are typically divided into sections differentiated by their motivic material, textures, tempi, key areas, and (at times) meters, just as in a Frescobaldi toccata (see Anthology 6). Whereas each section of a Frescobaldi toccata is marked only by a cadence, making the performer responsible for determining the correct tempo and character, Castello provides tempo markings (usually Adagio or Allegro) to delineate sections. In vocal works, contrasts are generated by changes in the text, often with sudden dissonances and tonal shifts. In Castello's "modern" sonatas (and Frescobaldi's toccatas) the contrasts arise from purely musical considerations, which provide the impetus for the often lengthier movements.

We can see some of the strategies that Castello uses to compose this longer work by comparing his somewhat more modern tonal language with that of his contemporaries. Unlike Frescobaldi's toccatas or the vocal works of Monteverdi, the Sonata No. 2 is quite diatonic. D minor is presented in a clear, unambiguous fashion, without the use of the *mollis–durus* contrasts that characterize the music of Monteverdi and Caccini (see Anthology 1, 2, 4, 5, and 9). The accompanying table shows the section divisions and Castello's modulations to key areas that are closely related from the perspective of modern tonal procedures. The first two sections are in D minor, with a move to F major (the relative major) in sections 3 and 5, interrupted by a brief Adagio section in the parallel major of D. The sixth section moves from the dominant

SECTION	MEASURES	TEMPO	KEY
1	1–23	Allegro	D minor
2	23–30	Adagio	D minor
3	31–48	Allegro (triple meter)	F major
4	49–51	Adagio (brief cadential passage)	D major
5	51–85	Allegro (with tremolo section)	F major
6	86–94	Allegro (with triplets)	A major to D minor
7	95–112	Adagio (subdivisions articulated at mm. 104 and 109 for lengthy IV–I cadence)	D minor to D major

A major back to D minor, and the final Adagio anchors the D minor via the subdominant, concluding, as was typical in the period, with a D major chord.

Much of the sonata's tension is conveyed through instrumental virtuosity and ornamentation—for instance, in the extensive passagework in all of the Allegro sections that flow easily in and out of the highly expressive Adagios. Although many of the ornaments are borrowed from vocal music, particularly those codified by Caccini in *Le nuove musiche*, such as the written-out trills in measures 106 and 109–110, there is no question that we are dealing with an entirely instrumental idiom. Regardless of which treble instrument might play this sonata, the writing goes far beyond the capabilities of the human voice in terms of range, technical difficulty, and the sheer length of the melodic lines. Castello generates such extended passages by combining a variety of melodic motives or formulas. The first section, for example, consists of different combinations and sequential treatments of ideas presented in measures 4–7, such as the triad and descending scale (m. 6) and the cadential figure with the trill (m. 7).

Castello employs some of his most innovative instrumental techniques in section 5. These include echo effects in measures 65–73 and tremolos in measures 74–85, which could be performed not only on the violin (with the bow) but also with the breath and tongue on a cornetto. The subsequent section (mm. 86–94) is also marked Allegro. The shift to a gigue-like series of triplets, along with the move to the dominant, provide a further intensification, leading to the final Adagio section. This virtuosic finish demands a high degree of expressivity, even including extra Adagio markings for the trills in measure 109.

8

JOHANN JACOB FROBERGER (1616-1667)

Libro quarto di toccate, ricercari, capricci, allemande, gigue, courante, sarabande: Suite in C Major, FbWV 612
Keyboard suite, 1656

Lamento

Sopra la dolorosa perdita della Real M^stà di FERDINANDO IV, Ré de Romani +c.

From Johann Jacob Froberger, *Oeuvres Complètes Pour Clavecin*, Vol. 1, ed. Howard Schott (Paris: Huegel, 1979). Reprinted by permission.

Gigue

Courante

Sarabande

Johann Jacob Froberger's C-Major Suite appears in an autograph manuscript entitled *Libro quarto di toccate, ricercari, capricci, allemande, gigue, courante, sarabande* (Fourth Book of Toccatas, Ricercars, Capriccios, Allemandes, Gigues, Courantes, Sarabandes). Compiled in 1656, the collection was presented to the Holy Roman Emperor Ferdinand III of Vienna, where the well-traveled Froberger was employed both in the middle and at the end of his career.

Froberger linked together these four dance movements in binary form and in the same key by placing them adjacent to one another in the manuscript. Such sets of dances and character pieces in the same key came to be known as suites later in the eighteenth century, but the term is actually not found in this manuscript. Froberger is often credited with codifying the genre of the Baroque suite, since he used many of the dances that would become standard in the eighteenth century. However, his ordering of the dances (allemande-gigue-courante-sarabande) is quite different from that of later composers, such as Bach, whose suites typically consisted of a core of dances (allemande-courante-sarabande-gigue) to which other dance genres known as *galanteries* (such as minuets, bourrées, and gavottes) might be added.

All four movements of Froberger's C-Major Suite are in binary form, the most common for dance movements, usually represented as ||:**A**:||:**B**:||. The first section moves to the dominant or, in the case of a movement in a minor key, the relative major, while the second section returns to the tonic key. Both sections are usually repeated. The style of keyboard writing for which Froberger was particularly renowned, the *style brisé* (broken style), breaks up a single musical line through arpeggiation or by notating the individual voices with slightly different rhythms so as to imitate the texture that is possible on the lute. (The style was also known as *style luthé*.) In measures 8–10 of the Gigue, for example, the chords over the D pedal are distributed in such a way as to create a two- and at times even three-voice texture in the right hand.

The opening movement, a slow and stately dance in duple meter, with light upbeat motives, is clearly an allemande, even though Froberger does not label it as such. The title alludes to the piece's extramusical significance: a lament "on the sorrowful loss of Ferdinand IV," referring to the eldest son of the Holy Roman Emperor Ferdinand III, who died of smallpox in 1654 at the age of 21. Froberger skillfully employs *style brisé*, prepared and unprepared dissonances, using rhythmic freedom, and poignant chromaticism to create a powerful expression of grief, despite the fact that the piece is in a major key. Indeed, he likely chose C major because, at a time when keyboard instruments were tuned in unequal temperaments, whereby some keys sounded more "in tune" than others, C major was the most consonant key; its purity may well have seemed appropriate to mourn the loss of a child.

The heightened expressivity is apparent in the very first measure. Unlike the eighth-note dominant upbeat that begins Arcangelo Corelli's allemande

(see Anthology 17) or the sixteenth-note anticipation of the tonic used by François Couperin to open *La ténébreuse* (see Anthology 18), Froberger's three-note
opening figure is both tonally and rhythmically ambiguous: he begins on the
leading tone B, settling on the tonic C (marked with a trill) on the weakest part
of the beat—the second sixteenth note—before landing on the third of the tonic
chord on the down beat. Even there, the melody dissipates with a gentle thirty-
second-note ascent to the G. Froberger then immediately gives us a variation
on that opening gesture, intensified with thirty-second notes (at the end of
m. 1), leading in measure 2 to a bold stepwise passage from C to G.

Among the intense rhetorical gestures in this first movement are the
numerous dotted or held notes that cascade into thirty-second notes (as in
m. 10) and the sigh motives in descending sixteenth-note skips in the right
hand (mm. 3, 8, and 15). The intensity increases in the **B** section: the explosive
descending scalar passage in measure 18 leads to the most dissonant passage
in the movement: the simultaneous sounding of F and E♮ against the B♮ in the
bass on beat 3, a sonority that is particularly jarring in the resonant middle
register of the harpsichord.

The most remarkable feature of the Lamento is the conclusion: an ascending three-octave C-major scale *after* the final cadence on the tonic chord,
which, quite remarkably, seems to complete the truncated C-major scales
in the opening measures. It is no coincidence that the C-major chord on the
downbeat of measure 25 is voiced identically with the one on the first beat of
measure 1, and that the last two notes of the movement are the same as the
first two, albeit two octaves higher. Scholars have speculated that Froberger
intended this scale to represent the ascent of the young Ferdinand's soul to
heaven, a point that is made explicit in the drawing of the clouds and sun in the
margin of the manuscript (see Fig. 4.6 in *Music in the Baroque*). By ending the
piece in the upper register with this recollection of the ambiguous opening,
Froberger seems to suggest that his lament, like Ferdinand's soul, will live on
eternally.

The remaining three movements provide excellent examples of the various dance types that would become standard in the Baroque suite. The Gigue
combines Italian and French styles: the typically Italianate upbeat figure and
compound meter are juxtaposed with French ornamentation and *style brisé*.
This mixture comes as no surprise in light of Froberger's travels and his
close connection to both Frescobaldi and Louis Couperin. The Courante, by
contrast, is totally "French": although it is notated uniformly in triple meter,
melodic and harmonic accents create passages in both compound duple and
compound triple. Measure 14, for instance, is in a strong $\frac{3}{2}$ meter, while $\frac{6}{4}$ is
equally pronounced in measure 15. The Sarabande, with its slow triple meter
and accentuated second beat, is typical of French and German sarabandes of
the seventeenth and eighteenth centuries.

9

CLAUDIO MONTEVERDI (1567–1643)

Vespro della Beata Vergine: *Duo Seraphim*
Sacred concerto, published 1610

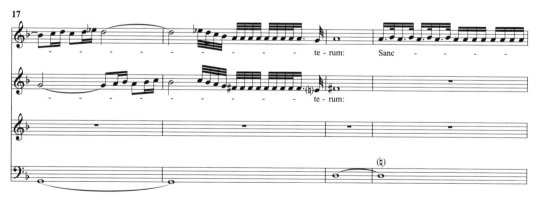

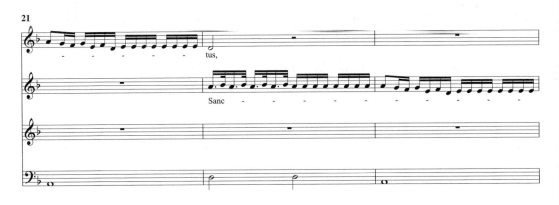

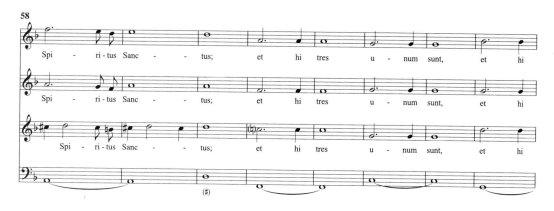

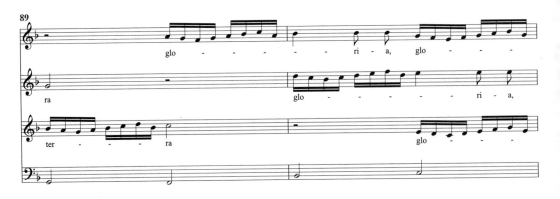

Duo seraphim clamabant alter ad alterum:	*Two seraphim called to one another:*
Sanctus, sanctus, Dominus Deus sabaoth.	*Holy, holy is the Lord of Hosts.*
Plena est omnis terra gloria eius.	*The whole earth is full of His glory.*
Tres sunt qui testimonium dant in coelo:	*There are three who bear witness in heaven:*
Pater, Verbum et Spiritus sanctus.	*the Father, the Word, and the Holy Spirit.*
Et hi tres unum sunt.	*And these three are one.*
Sanctus, sanctus, Dominus Deus sabaoth.	*Holy, holy is the Lord of Hosts.*
Plena est omnis terra gloria eius.	*The whole earth is full of His glory.*

During the summer of 1610, the assistant *maestro di cappella* in Mantua, Bassano Cassola, sent a report to the duke of Mantua, Ferdinando Gonzaga, that Claudio Monteverdi was "having printed an *a cappella* Mass for six voices of great studiousness and labour," based on themes from Nicholas Gombert's motet *In illo tempore*: "And he is also having printed psalms for the Vespers of the Madonna, with various and diverse manners of invention and of harmony—and all are on the cantus firmus—with the idea of coming to Rome this autumn to dedicate them to His Holiness."

The volume to which Cassola referred was arguably Monteverdi's most significant collection of sacred music. Published in 1610, while the composer was serving at the Gonzaga court, it was entitled "For the Most Holy Virgin, a Mass for Six Voices suitable for church choirs, and Vespers to be performed by diverse forces (together with some motets) suitable for chapels or chambers of princes. Works by Claudio Monteverdi, recently composed and dedicated to his Holiness Pope Paul V."

Perhaps conceived in answer to Giovanni Maria Artusi's criticisms of "O Mirtillo" and other alleged "monsters" by Monteverdi (see Anthology 1), the first of the 15 works included in the publication was a traditional six-voice mass based on a motet by Gombert. The fact that Monteverdi listed the motives drawn from the Renaissance composer's music indicates that he was self-consciously writing in the archaic style of the *prima prattica* (first practice). The remainder of the collection, however, which he labels inside the print as the *Vespro della Beata Vergine* (Vespers of the Blessed Virgin), includes some of Monteverdi's most progressive and intimate settings of devotional music, as well as some of his most brilliant writing for large performing forces.

Vespers took place in the early evening as part of the Divine Office, the cycle of religious rites performed throughout the day in Catholic institutions. It included the singing of psalms, alternating with antiphons (responses sung by the choir and the cantor), concluding with the recitation of the Magnificat (the canticle of the Virgin from Luke 1:46–55), and brief closing formulas.

Scholars have long wondered whether Monteverdi intended the collection to be used in its entirety for an actual Vespers service. In some respects,

Monteverdi follows traditional procedures. His psalm settings, for instance, each included a cantus firmus (a section of previously written chant, sung in long notes), around which Monteverdi structured the other choral parts, although he also employs Baroque *stile concertato*, the concerted style, in which one or more groups of instruments or voices *concert* or interact with one another. Monteverdi, however, does not place antiphons between the psalms, but rather intersperses sacred concertos composed in a distinctly modern style. (See Anthology 10 for an example of a sacred concerto by Heinrich Schütz.) Some scholars have speculated that Monteverdi never meant them to be performed as part of a Vespers service, while others have argued that he intended the sacred concertos to substitute for the usual antiphons.

The question of liturgical use becomes particularly complicated with "Duo Seraphim," since its text, unlike that of the other sacred concertos, is not associated with the Virgin Mary but rather with the feast of the Holy Trinity. However, the Trinity was a subject especially venerated by Monteverdi's patrons, the Gonzagas, so the inclusion of "Duo Seraphim" may not originally have been out of place at all. Regardless of its intended liturgical function, "Duo Seraphim" is a highly dramatic and masterful setting of excerpts from the books of Isaiah (6:3) and John (5:7). In the first part (lines 1–3, mm. 1–45), the two seraphim call out to each other, first together and then in alternation, using a highly ornate style reminiscent of Orpheus's plea to Pluto in Act 3 of Monteverdi's *L'Orfeo*. The cries of the seraphim, which are both beautiful and painful, are dramatized by a remarkable series of 2–3 suspensions in measures 10–14, which explode into cascades of melismas. Intelligibility of the text is less critical here than the awe-inspiring effects created by the overlapping voices of the two tenors and their lengthy, florid melodies punctuated by fully notated *trilli*—a popular ornament featuring rapidly repeating notes—that evoke the unimaginable music of the angels.

The shift to the Trinitarian text from the Gospel of St. John is dramatized by the addition of the third tenor in measure 46. The first tenor introduces the Father (m. 53), the second the Word (m. 55), while the third tenor's melisma on the word "et" (and, m. 57) prepares for all three to join together homophonically for the invocation of the Holy Spirit (mm. 58–60). Monteverdi further dramatizes the Trinitarian notion of three in one by having all three singers move from a triad to unison Gs over a IV–I cadence on C (mm. 61–64), subsequently heightening the effect by transposing this brief passage up a step (mm. 65–68).

The final section, from measure 69 on, appears at first to be merely a reprise of the musical material beginning in measure 10. However, by retaining the third tenor, Monteverdi transforms the material heard earlier. In measure 73, for instance, he supplies a third repetition of the florid "Sanctus" and with the entrance of the third tenor in measure 77, the texture becomes far richer and contrapuntally complex, particularly in his extended treatment of the word "gloria" (glory) beginning in measure 88, for which there is no equivalent in Part 1. The retention of the third voice in this final section not only enhances the sonic effect and enriches the counterpoint, but from a theological perspective provides a Christian reinterpretation of Isaiah 6:3, while perhaps invoking an even more-ancient tradition: the threefold repetition of the word "Sanctus" (Kadosh in the original Hebrew from Isaiah), which is an integral part of the Jewish liturgy.

10

HEINRICH SCHÜTZ (1585–1672)

Symphoniae sacrae, Book 1: *Fili mi, Absalon*, SWV 269
Sacred concerto, published 1629

Basso

Fi - li mi, fi - li mi, fi - li mi, fi - li mi, Ab - sa - lon,

Basso continuo

fi - li mi, fi - li mi, fi - li mi, Ab - sa - lon,

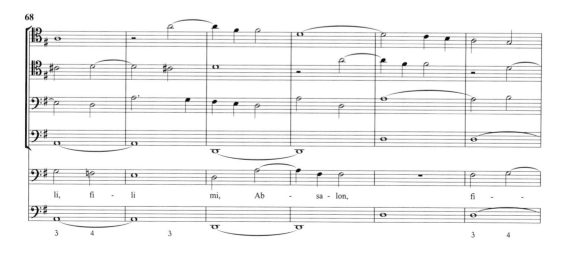

74

- li mi, fi - - - li mi.

81 Sinfonia
Trombone I

Trombone II

Trombone III

Trombone IV

Basso continuo

86

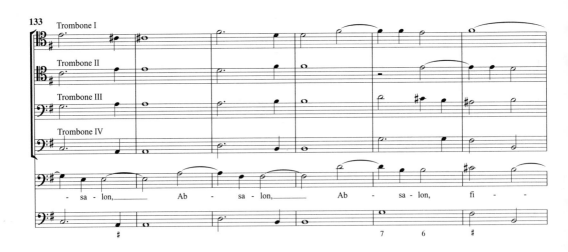

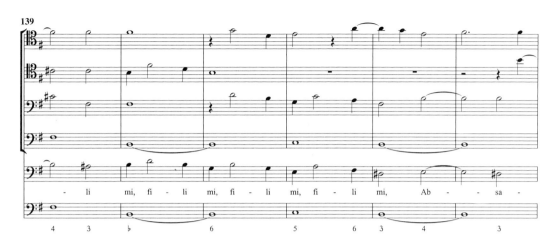

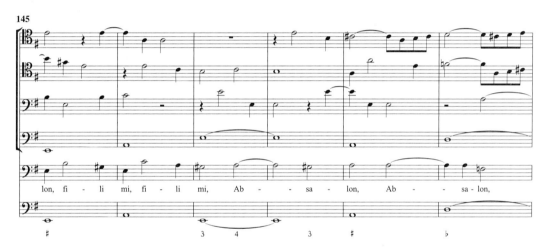

Fili mi, Absalon quis mihi tribuat ut ego   *My son, Absalom, would I had died for you,*
moriar pro te, Absalon, fili mi, fili mi.   *Absalom, my son, my son.*

In 1628, while the Thirty Years' War raged in northern Europe, Heinrich Schütz embarked on his second trip to Venice. It had been some 15 years since his last voyage to the Most Serene Republic, where as a young man he had studied with the great composer and organist Giovanni Gabrieli. This time Schütz had the opportunity to work with two of the most important composers of sacred music in Venice, Alessandro Grandi and Claudio Monteverdi. The fruits of his labor survive in Book 1 of his *Symphoniae sacrae* (Sacred Symphonies, 1629), a set of 20 Latin sacred concertos for voice and instruments (also often called motets), including "Fili mi, Absalon."

In setting King David's lament over the death of his son Absalom (2 Samuel 18:33), Schütz may have sought to emulate Renaissance motets, such as Josquin des Prez's well-known version. However, his rendition of this brief, moving Old Testament text is highly original. The scoring of the work—for four trombones, basso continuo, and solo bass—is typical of Schütz's innovative approach to instrumentation. The trombones, traditionally associated with death and the afterlife (as in Acts 3 and 4 of Monteverdi's *L'Orfeo*), create an appropriately somber atmosphere for David's grief.

"Fili mi, Absalon" can be divided into two parts, each beginning with a sinfonia (a term loosely applied to instrumental movements that introduce or are part of vocal works) for four trombones, followed by a section for solo bass and continuo, and concluding with the bass accompanied by the four trombones and continuo. Alternatively, the work also falls into two asymmetrical portions, defined by the shift from triple to duple meter at measure 53.

Schütz's sacred concerto differs from a number of the works we have studied thus far (for example, Monteverdi's "Duo seraphim," see Anthology 9) in that it does not achieve its expressive power by means of characteristic aspects of the *stile moderno,* such as chromaticism, unprepared dissonances, strings of suspensions, and unexpected tonal juxtapositions. In fact, with relatively few exceptions, "Fili mi, Absalon" is in a remarkably diatonic, even austere, A-minor/A-major tonality. Schütz plumbs the depths of David's sorrow through other means, in particular the rhythmic manipulation of the work's central motive—ascending and descending triads—with syncopations, augmentation (longer note values), diminution (shorter note values), and shifting meters. These devices, in addition to the novel instrumentation, enable Schütz not only to create an atmosphere of grandeur, mystery, and deep despair, but also to increase the tragic mood over the course of the piece.

The motive of a series of interlocking ascending triads on A, C, E is introduced in the opening sinfonia and taken up again by the solo bass in measure 43 (after the cadence on C major) in the trombone sinfonia, this time with the addition of G♯s that anchor this section fully in A major. Schütz's text setting further underscores the king's grief: the fourfold repetition of the phrase "fili mi" (my son) presents a man so frozen in his sorrow that he can barely bring himself to say his son's name. With the entrance of the trombones in measure 54, however, the name becomes an obsession. The shift to duple meter provides an increase in pacing and force. Schütz inverts the interval of the third that was so integral to the previous two sections, first stretching it temporally over the barline (mm. 54–57) and then expanding it intervallically to a fifth (mm. 61–62) and fourth (mm. 63–67).

The second sinfonia (mm. 81–107) features a more active rhythmic surface, quicker harmonic rhythm, and more generous use of sequences and suspensions, leading to the musical and dramatic core of the piece: David's expression of the desire to die in place of his son. This text inspires some of the most tonally adventurous moments in the work. The section begins (m. 108) on an E-major chord, the dominant of A major; as David utters the futile wish that he might have been the one to die, the harmony lands on a jarring F♯-major sonority (m. 113). The threefold repetition of the verb "moriar" inspires a sufficiently chromatic passage to lead to an equally unexpected F-major chord in measure 118. The surprises are still not over, as David's vocal line (in unison with the bass) descends stepwise a diminished fifth, forming the basis of a B-major sonority (m. 120). Such chromatic inflections and unexpected shifts between the *mollis* (flat) and *durus* (sharp) sonorities, reminiscent of Monteverdi's *L'Orfeo* (see Anthology 4), provide an apt expression of David's despair.

The final section provides a satisfying, if somber, conclusion to the work. The obsessive cries of Absalom's name on descending thirds return, now part of a single, unbroken utterance. In measures 140–43, David's repeated lamentations on "fili mi" are based on a free inversion of the opening motive, here a series of interlocking descending triads beginning on D, B, and A, made more emphatic with syncopation and bolstered by the trombones, which sometimes imitate and other times accompany the voice. We seem to have come full circle: the ascending triads that so mysteriously began the work in the trombone choir are inverted and given a new, albeit mournful, interpretation.

Schütz saves another expert touch for the end: anticipated by the octave descents in the third trombone in measures 147–48, David cries his son's name on a series of descending intervals—a third (mm. 149–50), a fifth (mm. 151–52), and an octave (mm. 153–54)—and comes to rest on the low A on which he began his lament. There is no respite from grief; if anything, it has become deeper and more forceful, indicating that the king is no closer to understanding or accepting his tragedy. With consummate mastery and eloquent simplicity, Schütz allows the listener both to witness and to participate in one of the most profound musical depictions of human sorrow.

11

GIACOMO CARISSIMI (1605–1674)

Jephte: Plorate colles
Oratorio, ca. 1648

go, e - go fi - li - a u - ni - ge - ni - ta mo - ri - ar et _____

non vi - vam. Ex - hor - re - sci - te ru - pes, ob - stu - pe - sci - te

col - les, val - les et ca - ver - nae in so - ni - tu hor - ri - bi - li re - so -

na - te, val - les et ca - ver - nae in so - ni - tu hor - ri - bi - li, in so - ni - tu hor -

ri - bi - li, re - so - na - te!

Echo

re - so -

re - so -

tasto solo

Plorate colles, dolete montes,
et in afflictione cordis mei
    ululate (*echo*: ululate).
Ecce moriar virgo et non potero
    morte mea meis filiis consolari.
Ingemiscite silvae, fontes et flumina
in interitu virginis lachrimate
    (*echo*: lachrimate).
Heu me dolentem in laetitia populi,
    in victoria Israel et gloria patris mei.

Ego sine filiis virgo, ego filia
    unigenita moriar et non vivam.
Exhorrescite rupes, obstupescite colles,
valles et cavernae in sonitu horribili
    resonate! (*echo*: resonate)
Plorate filii Israel, plorate virginitatem
    meam
et Jephte filiam unigentiam in carmine
    doloris lamentamini.

Weep, hills; mourn, mountains;
and, in the affliction of my heart,
    wail (echo: wail).
See, I shall die a virgin and I shall not be
    consoled by my children at my death.
Groan, forests, springs, and rivers,
weep for the death of a virgin
    (echo: weep).
Woe is me, sorrowful, amid the joy of the
    people in Israel's victory, and my father's glory.

I, without children, a virgin, I the only
daughter will die and not live.
Shudder, crags; hills, stand still;
valleys and caves, resound with horrible cries!
    (echo: resound)
Weep, children of Israel, bewail my virginity

and lament Jephtha's only daughter in a song
    of sorrow.

In all probability, Giacomo Carissimi's *Jephte* (Jephtha) was one of the Latin musical dramas based on scriptural themes that were heard at the Oratorio del Santissimo Crocifisso (Oratorio of the Most Holy Crucifix) in Rome. While Carissimi and his colleagues would not have described *Jephte* as an oratorio, the term is typically used to describe extended dramatic vocal compositions on sacred themes, such as Handel's *Saul* (see Anthology 24). Usually performed during Lent, oratorios employed a narrator, a chorus, and solo singers who represented individual characters. Although featuring religious themes, they used many of the musical strategies familiar from theatrical music to inspire devotional sentiments appropriate to the season, often with tragic overtones.

The biblical story of the warrior Jephtha was among the most popular topics for oratorios and cantatas in the Baroque. As told in the Book of Judges 11:1–40, Jephtha prays to God for victory in his battle with the Ammonites, vowing to sacrifice the first person he sees upon his return. This proves to have been a fatal error, for the women who greet the triumphant hero are led by none other than his daughter. The homecoming scene offers ample inspiration for the sudden changes in affect so treasured by Baroque composers: we hear the singing and dancing of the jubilant women, Jephtha's exclamations of horror at seeing his daughter and her anguish at the harsh decree, and the sympathetic laments of the Israelites as the daughter implores them to "bewail my virginity." Although in Carissimi's work the daughter presumably goes to her death, it is worth noting that the treatment of the same story in Handel's final oratorio, *Jephtha* (1751), has a happy ending: the daughter is rescued by an angel and sings a duet with her beloved.

One of the most interesting features of Carissimi's *Jephte* is the distribution of the vocal parts. The role of the warrior is sung by a tenor and his nameless daughter (she is only called Filia) is set for soprano, but was likely performed by a castrato or male falsettist. The part of the narrator or *historicus*, however, is not written for a single voice. Rather, it is divided between a solo alto, bass, and a four-part ensemble that function much like the chorus in Greek tragedies.

The excerpt included here is from the tragic end of the tale—the daughter's lament over her impending death, which is echoed by the sympathetic cries of the children of Israel. Carissimi uses a number of *stile moderno* techniques in this moving utterance: dissonances, cross-relations, suspensions, movement between the flat and sharp sides of the tonal spectrum, and the rhythmic freedom that we associate with recitative. One of Carissimi's most effective techniques was to repeat sections of text (and the associated melodic ideas), which were further intensified through transposition to different pitch levels. This technique is analogous to the rhetorical strategies used during this period by priests, who sought to move believers to a higher spiritual plane by artfully changing the volume, pitch, and pace of their speech.

In the opening measures, the rhetorical effect is enhanced through the repetition of the word "plorate" (weep), the unexpected addition of B♭ in the A-minor environment (m. 1), and the cross-relations with the E-major sonority (m. 2). In the very next phrase (mm. 3–4) we hear a variation of the same motivic idea, now transposed up a fifth for "dolete" (mourn). For the next line ("and, in the affliction of my heart, wail"), Carissimi transposes the passage in measures 5–8 up a fourth in measures 9–12, thus heightening the dramatic impact. Note how the melisma on "ululate" (wail) not only illustrates the wailing with heartrending accuracy, but also recalls the suspension and lower neighbor note from the "cry" of the opening phrase. Carissimi will use similar compositional strategies throughout the movement.

Jephte also includes a remarkable example of the echo effects that intrigued many seventeenth-century composers, including Arcangelo Corelli (see Anthology 17). The imitation between the soprano voices in measures 14–15 creates a kind of reverberation, prompting the listener to imagine the daughter sobbing alone in the mountains. The melismatic, echoing cries of the chorus in fact provide the structural pillars of this otherwise quite free, impassioned recitation. The final six-voice chorus (not included here) is both a lament and a sacred rite. Carissimi banishes the dissonances and intrusive B♭s and introduces dotted rhythms for the ostinato-like repetitions of "lamentamini" (lament). Thus is the listener urged to accept the daughter's sacrifice with grace and faith in God.

12

FRANCESCO CAVALLI (1602–1676)

Giasone, Act 3, scene 21: *Infelice, ch'ascolto?*
Opera, 1649

l'em - pio de - si - o.____ Sì, sì, sì, sì, ti - ran - no mi - o, fe - ri - sci a par - te a

par - te que - ste mem - bra a - bor - ri - te, sbra - na - mi a po - co a po - co que - ste car - ni in - fe - li - ci, a - na - to - miz - za il

se - no, stra - zia - mi a tuo pia - ce - re, mar - ti - riz - za - mi i sen - si, e'l mio len - to, len -

- to, len - to mo - ri - re pro - lun - ghi a me il tor - men - to, a te il gio - i - re.____

Ma se d'es - ser ma - ri - to l'a - do - ra - te me - mo - rie al fin per - de - sti, fa' ch'il no - me di pa - dre fra

le tue cru-del-ta-de in-tat-to re - sti.___ Non ti scor-dar, Gia - son, che pa - dre

se - i, e che son di te par-te i par - ti mie - i.___ Se leg-ge di na-

tu - ra ob-bli-ga a gl'a-li-men-ti an - co le fie - re, fa' che ma-no pie-to-sa gli

som-mi-ni-stri al-men vit-to men-di - co, E non sof-frir, ch'i tuoi scet-tra-ti fi - gli

per la fa-me lan-guen - te spi-rin l'al - me in-no-cen - ti.

Re - gi - na, E - ge - o, a -

mi - ci, sup - pli - ca - te per me que - - sto, que - sto cru -

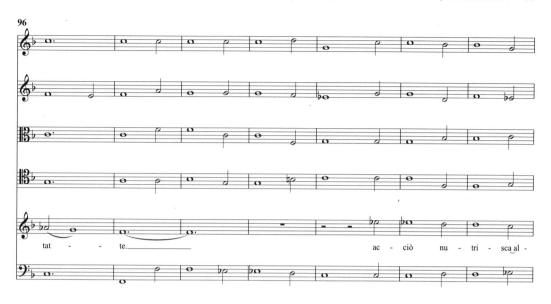

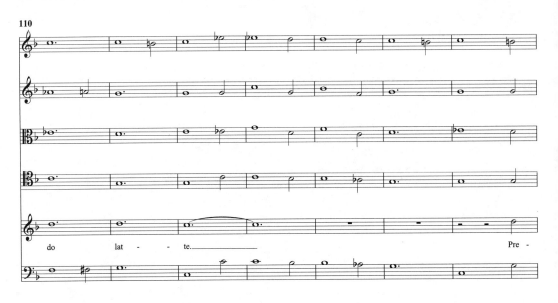

do   lat -   - te._____   Pre -

ga -   te - lo   pie - to - si   che   que - gl'an - ge - li in - fan -   -   -

ti as - si - sti - no ai mar - ti - ri del - la ma - dre tra - di - ta, e che ad o - gni fe -

ri - ta che im-pri - me - rà nel mio pu - di - co pet - to be - vi - no quel - li il san - gue mio stil -

129

lan - te, ac - ciò ch'ei tra - pas - san - do nel - le lor pu - re ve - ne in lor s'in - car - ni, on - de il lor se - no in qual - che

133

par - te si - a tom - ba in - no - cen - te al - l'in - no - cen - za mi - a.

Infelice, ch'ascolto?
Non t'affannar, Giasone,
che se la vita mia
fu, come ben intesi,
un aborto d'errori
che produce il tuo duolo,
vengo a sacrificarla a' tuoi furori.
S'io perivo trà l'acque,
una morte sì breve
forse non appagava i tuoi rigori;
ma se viva son io,
rallegrati, o crudele,
giacché potrai con replicate morti
sfogar del fiero cor l'empio desio.
Sì, sì, tiranno mio,
ferisci a parte, a parte
queste membra aborrite,
sbranami a poco, a poco
queste carni infelici,
anatomizza il seno,
straziami a tuo piacere,
martirizzami i sensi,
e'l mio lento morire
prolunghi a me il tormento, a te il gioire.
Ma se d'esser marito
l'adorate memorie al fin perdesti,
fa' ch'il nome di padre
fra le tue crudeltade intatto resti.
Non ti scordar, Giason, che padre sei
e che son di te parte i parti miei.
Se legge di natura
obbliga a gl'alimenti anco le fiere,

fa' che mano pietosa
gli somministri almen vitto mendico,
e non soffrir ch'i tuoi scettrati figli
per la fame languente
spirin l'alme innocenti.

Regina, Egeo, amici,
supplicate per me questo crudele,
che nel ferirmi ei lasci
queste mammelle dai suoi colpi intatte,
acciò nutrisca almeno i figli miei

Unhappy one, what do I hear?
Do not concern yourself, Jason,
for if my life
(as I well understand) was
a freak accident
that caused your sorrow,
I come to sacrifice it to your fury.
If I had died in the waters,
a death so quick
might not have satisfied your severity;
but since I am alive,
rejoice, o cruel one,
for now you can with repeated deaths
vent the evil desire of your wicked heart.
Yes, yes, my tyrant,
Tear to pieces, to pieces
these hated limbs,
dismember bit by bit
my unhappy flesh,
dissect my breast,
lacerate me for your pleasure,
make a martyr of my senses,
and in my slow death
prolong my torment, and your joy.
But if in the end you have lost
the adored memories of being a husband,
let the name of father remain
intact among your cruelties.
Don't forget, Jason, that you are a father,
and that they are partly yours and partly mine.
If the law of nature
obligates even wild animals to nurture their
 young,
let your merciful hand
administer to them at least a beggar's provisions,
and do not let your scepter-bearing sons,
languishing with hunger,
relinquish their innocent souls.

Queen, Aegeus, friends,
plead on my behalf with this cruel one,
that in wounding me he leaves
these breasts intact from his blows,
so the cold milk from the dead maternal breast
 can

del morto sen materno un freddo latte.	*still nourish my sons.*
Pregatelo pietosi	*Beg him mercifully*
che quegl'angeli infanti	*that these angelic children*
assistino ai martiri	*watch the martyrdom*
della madre tradita,	*of their betrayed mother,*
e che ad ogni ferita	*and that for every wound*
che imprimerà nel mio pudico petto	*that is to be stamped on my pure breast,*
bevino quelli il sangue mio stillante,	*they might drink of my dripping blood,*
acciò che'ei trapassando	*so that, in passing*
nelle lor pure vene, in lor s'incarni,	*into their pure veins, it will become part of their flesh,*
Onde il lor seno in qualche parte sia	*and their breasts will in some way be part*
tomba innocente, all'innocenza mia.	*of the innocent tomb to my innocence.*
Addio terra, addio sole,	*Farewell earth, farewell sun,*
addio regina amica, amici addio,	*farewell queen, my friend; farewell friends,*
addio scettri, addio patria, addio mia prole.	*farewell scepters, farewell my homeland, farewell my children.*
Sciolta la madre vostra	*Your mother, released*
dal suo terrestre velo	*from her earthly form,*
attenderà di rivedervi in cielo.	*will wait to see you in heaven.*
Venite [omai, venite,	*Come now, come*
figli miei,] cari pegni,	*my children, dearest pledges,*
tempo è ch'io vi consegni	*the time has come for me to relinquish you*
all'adorato mostro	*to this beloved monster,*
ch'è carnefice mio e padre vostro.	*who is my executioner and your father.*
Figli, v'attendo e moro;	*Children, I await you and die,*
e te Giason, benché omicida, adoro.	*and you, Jason, even though a murderer, I love you.*

Francesco Cavalli's *Giasone* (1649), one of the relatively few Venetian operas to be staged repeatedly in the seventeenth century, demonstrates the playful and often irreverent way in which composers and librettists approached the ancient sources that inspired many of their operas. The libretto by Giacinto Cicognini combines two different myths about the hero Jason (Giasone): one in which he gains the Golden Fleece with the assistance of the sorceress Medea, and another from an earlier episode in his life in which he lands on the island of Lemnos, meets Queen Hypsipyle (Isifile), impregnates her, and then abandons her. In the opera, Jason is torn between these two women: Medea, who uses her magic power to help him complete his quest (and who has borne him twins), and his former lover Hypsipyle, the mother of another set of twins fathered by Jason, who spends much of the opera lamenting his infidelity and her fate as an abandoned woman.

In the final scene of the opera, Hypsipyle, who has just learned that her unfaithful husband Jason tried to rid himself of her by having her murdered, confronts him and Medea, her two children by her side. Her ensuing monologue is a dramatic and musical tour de force, in which the rejected queen uses a broad range of vocal styles—from impassioned recitative to a lament-style aria, accompanied by strings—to shame her former lover. The rhythmically flexible vocal line thus reflects the subtle nuances of her speech. Note, for instance, as she focuses on Jason's cruelty (mm. 21–26), that Cavalli concentrates on the sharp (*durus*) key of E minor, using *stile concitato* (as she does often in this monologue) to express her anger (mm. 22–23), culminating in an ascent into the upper register for the cadence in measure 26 as she decries his wicked heart.

Cavalli places Hypsipyle's fervent plea that Jason tear her limb from limb into relief by slowing down the harmonic rhythm and setting the most violent part of her speech over a C-major sonority (colored with a dissonant fourth in m. 32) with vivid text painting: *stile concitato* depicts the painful tortures Jason will inflict (mm. 29–35), while sustained notes dramatize the slow death she imagines for herself (mm. 36–41). Hypsipyle softens as she reminds Jason of his responsibilities as father to her children (m. 51); the shift in mood is represented by the change to a one-flat key signature and more lyrical vocal style, culminating in an ascending chromatic passage (mm. 58–68) and a dramatic octave plunge to low D (m. 70).

In the aria that forms the second section, Hypsipyle makes her case to the entire cast of the opera. Lest we imagine that this is not a lament, Cavalli, adding pairs of violins and violas (omitted in some of the surviving manuscripts) and shifting to triple meter, gives us two statements of a descending minor tetrachord (mm. 71–78), reminiscent of Monteverdi's lamenting nymph (see Anthology 5). Hypsipyle pleads not for her own life but for her offspring, and asks (with considerable theatrical aplomb) that Jason preserve her breasts so that the children might continue to be nourished even after her death. In measure 123, anger once again takes over and the strings lend an air of gravity to another vehement recitative, composer and librettist saving for last the gruesome imagery of her children drinking her blood, their breasts thus serving as an "innocent tomb to [her] innocence." As the strings fall silent in measure 138, Hypsipyle moves to a highly lyrical recitative, or arioso, and—with more than a touch of high drama—bids farewell to the assembled company, emulating both the language and style that Monteverdi's Orpheus had used as he contemplated his trip to the underworld (see Anthology 4).

In the end, Hypsipyle, unlike many abandoned women in opera, gets what she wants: Jason, utterly humiliated, agrees to return to his former lover. But how seriously we should take this remarkable lament remains an open question. Does Hypsipyle really expect Jason to kill her or starve their children? What is indisputable is that Cavalli's heroine is a brilliant rhetorician whose eloquence proves more powerful than even Medea's magic.

Armide, Act 5, scene 5: *Le perfide Renaud me fuit*
Opera, 1686

Armide alone

From Jean-Baptiste Lully, *Oeuvres Complètes*, series 3, Vol. 14, *Armide*, ed. Lois Rosow, text ed. Jean-Nodel Laurenti (Hildesheim: Georg Olms, 2003). Reprinted by permission.

20

suit.   Il me lais - se mou-ran - te,   Il veut que je pe - ris - se.   A re-gret je re-voy la clar-

5♭   ♭   5♭

24

-té   qui me luit;   L'hor - reur de l'é - ter - nel - le Nuit   Ce - de à l'hor-reur de mon su - -

7   6   ♯   6   6
     4   4♯
                   2

27

-pli - - ce.   Le per - fi - de Re-naud me fuit,   Tout per - fi - de qu'il est, mon lâ - che cœur   le

6   6   6♯   ♯   6   ♯   6 6♯ ♭   6♯

suit.

Quand le Bar-ba-re es-toit en ma puis-

-san - ce, Que n'ay - je crû la Hai-ne et la Ven-gean - ce! Que n'ay - je sui-vy leurs trans-ports! Il m'es-

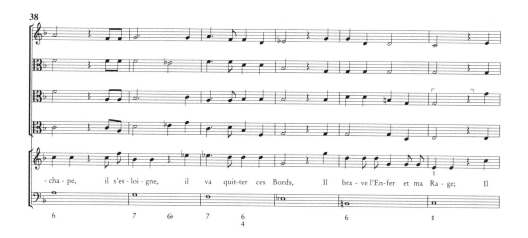

-cha - pe, il s'es - loi - gne, il va quit-ter ces Bords, Il bra - ve l'En-fer et ma Ra - ge; Il

est de-ja prés du Ri-va-ge, Je faits pour m'y trais-ner d'i-nu-ti- - les ef - forts.

Prélude

tiens son cœur per - fi - de... Ah!   je l'im-mo-le à ma fu-reur, je l'im-mo-le à ma fu-

Lentement

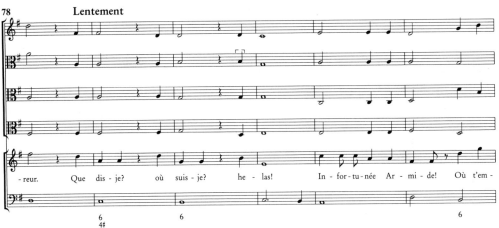

-reur.   Que dis-je?   où suis-je?   he - las!   In-for-tu-née Ar-mi-de!   Où t'em-

Vite

-por - te u-ne a - veu - gle er-reur?   L'es - poir de la ven-gean-ce est le seul qui me

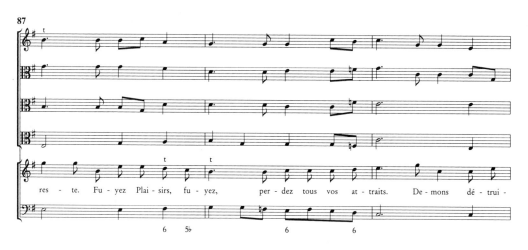

res - te. Fu - yez Plai - sirs, fu - yez, per - dez tous vos at - traits. De - mons dé - trui -

- sez ce Pa - lais. Fu - yez Plai - sirs, fu - yez, per - dez tous vos at - traits. De - mons, de - mons, dé - trui -

- sez, dé - trui - sez ce Pa - lais. L'es - poir de la ven - gean - ce est le seul qui me res - te. Par - tons, et s'il se

peut   que mon a-mour fu - nes - te De-meu-re en-se-ve-ly dans ces lieux   pour ja - mais.

The demons destroy the enchanted palace, and Armida departs on a flying chariot.

Prélude
Très Vite

Symphonie

End of the fifth and final act

Le perfide Renaud me fuit;
tout perfide qu'il est, mon lâche coeur
    le suit.
Il me laisse mourante, il veut que
    je périsse.

A regret je revois la clarté qui me luit;
l'horreur de l'éternelle nuit
cède à l'horreur de mon supplice.
Le perfide Renaud me fuit;
tout perfide qu'il est, mon lâche coeur
    le suit.
Quand le barbare était en ma puissance,
que n'ai-je cru la haine et la vengeance!
Que n'ai-je suivi leurs transports!
Il m'échappe, il s'éloigne, il va quitter
    ces bordes.
Il brave l'Enfer et ma rage.
Il est déjà près du ravage.
Je fais pour m'y traîner d'inutiles efforts.

Traître, attends. . . . Je le tiens . . . je
    tiens son coeur perfide.
Ah! Je l'immole à ma fureur. . . .
Que dis-je! Où suis-je, hélas!
    Infortunée Armide!
Où t'emporte une aveugle erreur?
L'espoir de la vengeance est le seul
    qui me reste.
Fuyez, plaisers, fuyez, perdez tous
    vos attraits.
Démons, déstruisez ce palais.
Partons, et s'il se peut, que mon
    amour funeste
demeure enseveli dans ces lieux
    pour jamais.

The perfidious Renaud flees from me;
though he is entirely perfidious, my weak heart
    follows him.
He leaves me dying, he wants me to perish.

Regretfully, I see again the light beckoning me;
the horror of eternal night
gives way to the horror of my torture.
The perfidious Renaud flees from me;
though he is entirely perfidious, my weak heart
    follows him.
When the cruel one was in my power,
why did I spurn hatred and vengeance?
Why did I not follow their wishes?
He escapes me, he travels away from me,
he is going to leave these shores.
He braves Hell and my fury.
He is already near the shore.
My efforts to drag myself there are useless.

Traitor, wait. . . . I possess him . . . I hold his
    perfidious heart.
Ah! I consume him with my fury. . . .
What am I saying? Where am I, alas?
    Unfortunate Armide!
Where does your blind error lead you?
Vengeance is the only hope I have left!

Flee, pleasures, flee, lose all your attractions.

Demons, destroy this palace.
Let us depart and, if possible, let my fatal love

remain buried in this place forever.

The text underlay in the score presents the spellings that were commonly used in seventeenth-century France. These have been modernized in the poetic text.

For much of his career, Jean-Baptiste Lully enjoyed a close personal relationship with King Louis XIV, creating court ballets and comedies (the latter in partnership with Molière) that were a central part of musical life at the

French court. Although Lully had long claimed that opera was impossible in the French language, he collaborated with the librettist Philippe Quinault to develop a style that took account of its unique features, incorporating as well the French passion for dance. They also chose topics that reflected the requisite heroic virtues for a ruler who was involved in numerous military conflicts.

On the surface, the story of *Armide*, Lully's fourteenth and final complete *tragédie en musique*, would appear to suit Louis's political goals quite well; in fact, the king chose it from among three options offered by Quinault. Drawn from Torquato Tasso's epic *Gerusalemme liberata* (Jerusalem Delivered), the story of the encounter between the Christian knight Rinaldo (Renaud) and the sorceress Armida (Armide) was popular not only in Italy but also in England (see Anthology 23 for Handel's treatment of the legend in his opera *Rinaldo*) as well as in France, where it had been the subject for two court ballets, one featuring Louis XIII (*La délivrance de Renaud ; 1617*) and another created for Louis XIV (*Ballet des Amours déguisés*). By the time Lully completed *Armide*, however, his relationship with Louis XIV had deteriorated, partly as a result of the composer's involvement in a sexual scandal. The opera was therefore performed first at the Paris Opéra, rather than at Versailles. Lully noted that of all his operas *Armide* was the one "with which the public seemed most satisfied," but it was likely never seen by the king.

In the opera's final scene, the hero Renaud, after having been captured and enchanted by the sorceress Armide (who, having fallen in love with him, could not bring herself to kill him), has broken free of her spell and escaped. The scene opens with a G-minor prelude for five-part string ensemble and continuo, initially in duple meter and marked "doux" (sweet or soft), intimating that Armide—at least for the moment—is less the vengeful sorceress than the abandoned lover. (The instrument designations that are shown in parentheses in the score reflect the typical string scoring in seventeenth-century France. The *dessus* or top line was played by the violin; the middle three parts were played by small, medium, and larger violas respectively, while a bass violin, in the range of the cello, was part of the continuo group.) The orchestra plays a vital role throughout the scene, not only accompanying all of Armide's utterances but also depicting much of the dramatic action. (Compare the excerpt from Cavalli's *Giasone* in Anthology 12, where the orchestra plays a much smaller role.)

Lully's setting of Quinault's eloquent poetry brings to the fore the conflict between Armide's love for Renaud and her desire for vengeance. Much of the emotional tension results from Lully's manipulation of the ever-pliant French recitative, so carefully crafted to suit Quinault's poetry. The different phrase lengths and shifting meters accommodate the inherently nonmetrical nature of the poetry and the variations in the number of syllables in each verse. Armide's first two lines, which frame the opening part of the monologue, epitomize her internal conflict. For the initial cry "Le perfide Renaud me fuit" (The perfidious Renaud flees from me), Armide boldly ascends to high G, remaining in the upper part of her range for the repetition of "perfide" in line 2. Yet she fails to sustain either her anger or the pitch level, descending almost meekly as she invokes her weakened heart on the downbeat of measure 20. What is perhaps most unexpected about the ensuing section is that Armide sings in symmetrical phrases (for example, mm. 33–35 and 42–44), avoiding angry outbursts. Her obsessive even thinking leads her to repeat the text and music of the opening two lines in measures 27–30; Armide is trapped by her emotions and seems paralyzed, unwilling or unable to use her magic powers, her emotional anguish heightened by the accompanying strings and continuo.

With the running eighth notes of the second orchestral prelude, in G major (mm. 50–64), the French version of the *stile concitato*, Armide seems to have broken out of her self-imposed prison. Breathlessly—as suggested by the sharp sixteenth-note upbeats—she tries to hold the traitor's heart (mm. 65–67), only to be interrupted by a moment of introspection (mm. 79–84), marked "Lentement" (slowly) in the score. The change in tempo to "Vite" (fast) betokens her recognition that her only hope lies in vengeance. As she returns to the upper register and calls upon the demons to destroy the palace, the formality of her final speech is reflected in the use of alexandrines, the 12-syllable lines used in French spoken tragedy.

The opera ends with a third instrumental prelude, to be played "Très Vite" (very fast): rapid-fire scales depict both the destruction of the palace and Armide's flight on her chariot. Renaud may escape from the clutches of the evil sorceress, but it is Armide, unrepentant and unpunished, who has the final word—a subversive, somewhat daring ending on the part of the composer and librettist that might well have brought displeasure to Louis XIV.

14

HENRY PURCELL (1659–1695)

King Arthur, Act 3: *What ho!* and *What power art thou*
Dramatick Opera, 1691

What Ho! Thou Genius

What ho! what ho! thou ge-nius of this isle; what ho! what ho!_____

_____ what ho! Liest__ thou a-sleep__ be-neath those hills of snow? What ho! what ho! what

ho! Stretch_____ out thy la - zy limbs. A-wake, a-wake, a-wake! And win-ter from thy

fur-ry man - tle shake: A-wake, a - wake!__ and win-ter from thy fur-ry man - tle shake.

What Power Art Thou

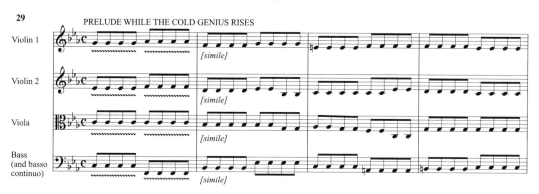

41

slow____ From beds____ of e - ver - last - - ing snow?____

45

See'st____ thou not____ how stiff,____ how stiff____ and won - drous

49

old,____ Far, far____ un - fit____ to bear____ the bit - ter cold,____

I can scarce - ly move___ or draw___ my breath,___ can scarce - ly move___ or draw___ my

breath?___ Let me, let me, let me freeze___ a - gain,___ Let me, let me freeze___ a - gain to

death, let me, let me, let me freeze___ a - gain to death

CUPID

What ho, thou Genius of this isle, what ho!
Liest thou asleep beneath those Hills of Snow?
Stretch out thy Lazy Limbs: Awake, awake,
And Winter from thy Furry Mantle Shake.

COLD GENIUS

What power art thou, who from below,
Hast made me rise, unwillingly and slow,
From beds of everlasting snow?
See'st thou not how stiff and wondrous old,
Far unfit to bear the bitter Cold,
I can scarcely move or draw my breath;
Let me, let me, Freeze again to death.

~~~

A work entitled *King Arthur* might conjure up visions of Lancelot, Guinevere, and the sword Excaliber, but Henry Purcell's Dramatick Opera (as the genre was dubbed by the poet, John Dryden) defies such expectations. The story focuses on an early episode in the life of the English monarch—his battles with the Saxon king Oswald—with no mention of the famous Knights of the Round Table. Although continental Europeans would not have considered *King Arthur* an opera (thus such works have often incorrectly been described as semi-operas), the English certainly did, since spoken dialogue was a vital part of their musical-theater tradition. In fact, the central serious characters in *King Arthur*, such as the king and his beloved Princess Emmeline, speak but never sing. Music is, for the most part, reserved for the magical realm of the sorcerers Merlin and Osmond (good and evil respectively), nymphs, shepherds, and Cupid, the god of love.

One of the elements that makes Dramatick Opera different from conventional operas is the alternation between the worlds of speech and song. We see something of how this balance works in the Frost Scene that opens Act 3. At this point in the play, the evil Osmond has abducted Princess Emmeline. When she refuses his advances, he declares that his love will thaw her. Osmond demonstrates the point by striking the ground with his magic wand and presenting a musical scene that features the mysterious Cold Genius, who has put all of Britain under a deep freeze. This initiates a lengthy sequence of airs, choruses, and dances—beginning with the section included here—which, much like Lully's *Armide* (see Anthology 13) and other French operas of the period, is organized in a modular fashion that accommodated both the flow of the drama and the necessity of introducing song and dance.

The musical portion of the scene begins with an orchestral prelude dominated by an offbeat, jagged sixteenth-note motive, which brings to mind the ice forming over the earth. Cupid's verse "What ho!" is a stellar example of the lyricism and expressivity of Purcell's recitative. The varied settings of the phrases "What ho!" and "Awake, awake!" provide musical unity and are balanced by illustrative vocalizations, such as the stepwise descending phrase on "stretch out thy lazy limbs" (mm. 21–22), with an unexpected B♭ teasingly coloring the word "lazy."

The most remarkable passage in Act 3—and perhaps the entire opera—is the air "What Power Art Thou" sung by the Cold Genius. It is accompanied by a series of repeated eighth-note chords, marked with squiggly lines calling for tremolos (the four notes were likely played by a single bow stroke), depicting icy earth and its shivering inhabitants. Purcell dramatizes the gradual emergence of the Genius not only with the tremolos but also with a somewhat unusual sequence of chords, colored with frequent ascending and descending chromatic motion in both the vocal and orchestral parts. In crafting the chordal accompaniment for the remarkable chromatic scalar passages sung by the Cold Genius, Purcell uses somewhat atypical voice-leading, often eschewing root-position triads, so that the chords seem to move almost imperceptibly from one to another sonority. This is apparent, for instance, in the remarkable climactic ascending passage as the Cold Genius climbs to the E♭ at the top of his range in measures 53–57. The journey seems to exhaust him, giving credence to his claim that he can scarcely breathe. This is the most dissonant moment in the entire work. Note, for instance, the shocking clash between the repeated Ds in the vocal part and the diminished triad in the orchestra on the downbeat of measure 58. The air concludes as the vocal line descends chromatically a final time.

Purcell does not, however, allow us to take the Cold Genius's fate too seriously. In the C-major air for Cupid that follows (not included here), with its jovial refrain, icy-cold chromaticism is banished in favor of warming diatonic harmonies, and playful syncopations provide an antidote to the Genius's four-square rhythms. Having thus disposed of the Cold Genius, Cupid now calls forth all the people to embrace love, leading to the "Frost Chorus," in which the entire chorus, on repeated eighth notes (with occasional tremolo markings), sings of quivering, trembling, and chattering teeth. Happily, Cupid provides the requisite heat. After the chorus joins in singing "'Tis love that has warm'd us," they dance. Once the music has ended, attention turns back to Emmeline, who is saved from Osmond's advances in the nick of time as the wizard is called off to rescue one of his evil spirits.

15

ANTONIO VIVALDI (1678–1741)

Concerto for Viola d'amore and Lute,
RV 540: Movement 1, Allegro
Concerto, 1740

124

129

168

176

On March 21, 1740, the crown prince of Saxony-Poland, Friedrich Christian, paid a visit to Santa Maria della Pietà, the Venetian orphanage where Antonio Vivaldi worked for much of his career. The authorities at the Pietà put on a special evening of musical entertainment in the prince's honor. The concert hall was decorated with golden brocade and lit with chandeliers and torches, and a stage was erected for the performance of a *serenata* (evening entertainment) entitled *Il coro delle muse* (The Chorus of the Muses). The "muses" of the Pietà—its famed female instrumentalists—demonstrated their skill by performing a sinfonia as a prelude and three concertos between the sections of the serenata. All four compositions, including the Concerto for Viola d'amore and Lute, RV 540, were bound together in a manuscript that was presented to Friedrich Christian and is now housed in the Saxon State Library in Dresden.

Vivaldi's gift for exploring novel instrumental sonorities is particularly evident in this brilliant double concerto. The viola d'amore, with its flat back, bears a certain resemblance to the viol, or "gamba" (leg), family of string instruments. Unlike viols, however, it has no frets on the fingerboard and rests on the player's arm, both attributes of the violin family. A significant feature of the viola d'amore (Italian for "love viol") is its two sets of strings, of which one is bowed while the other sounds "sympathetically." The sympathetic vibrations create a shimmering sonic halo that enriches the basic sound of the instrument and adds emotive power in special passages. Bach used a pair of viole d'amore at strategic dramatic moments in the *St. John Passion* (see Anthology 25)—for example, in the bass arioso "Betrachte, meine seele" (Ponder, my soul) and the tenor aria "Erwäge, wie sein blutgefärnter Rücken" (Consider how his blood-tinged back), in which the singers bemoan the flogging of Jesus prior to the Crucifixion.

In composing for the women at the Pietà, Vivaldi frequently employed unusual instruments, thus taking full advantage of his skilled players. Of his more than 500 concertos for various combinations of instruments, no fewer than eight feature the viola d'amore. But the soft-voiced lute rarely appeared in concertos as a solo instrument, making the Concerto for Viola d'amore and Lute all the more exceptional.

Vivaldi is usually credited with standardizing both the form of the three-movement Baroque concerto and the "ritornello form" typically used in the first and last movements. In ritornello form, an orchestral ritornello or refrain, played by the full orchestra, alternates with free sections dominated by one or more soloists. The solo sections often borrow motivic material from the ritornello, but the basic principle is one of contrast between the full orchestra and the soloists, who are usually accompanied by a reduced orchestra or just the continuo. (In the first movement of RV 540, the solo instruments are, unusually, supported only by first and second violins.)

Like many of his contemporaries, Vivaldi structured most of his ritornelli in three sections. The first section clearly establishes the tonic key, often with arpeggios, scales, and other figurations, cadencing on the dominant or relative major leading to a second contrasting section, in which the tension is maintained by harmonic or melodic sequences. The final section brings the listener back to the home key. The ritornello is typically heard in its entirety only at the beginning and end of the movement, with fragments played internally.

Although Vivaldi had spent decades establishing these conventions, in the first movement of the Concerto for Viola d'amore and Lute he treats the opening segment of the ritornello in an entirely original fashion. Rather than firmly establishing D minor at the outset, the rhythmic displacement between the upper strings on the one hand and the viola and basso continuo on the other subverts the sense of the tonic. The first root-position tonic chord occurs only on the last eighth note of measure 1. In fact, we have to wait until the end of the ritornello (m. 30) for a tonic cadence on a strong beat in the orchestra.

The first strong statement of any key area is that of the relative major in measures 8–16 (labeled in the accompanying diagram as an extension to the first section of the ritornello). This compensates for the tonal and rhythmic instability of the opening measures. Of particular note is the contrasting rhythmic character of the material in measures 12–13, which Vivaldi reserves for the first and last appearances of the ritornello: the continuo and viola take up the dotted pattern, providing a contrast to the repeated thirty-second-note undulating figures in the upper strings. Observe how Vivaldi carefully orchestrates this so that the sixteenth notes in the viola and continuo sound during the sixteenth-note rests in the upper voices. The second and third sections of the ritornello are largely straightforward: ritornello b, which begins on the upbeat to measure 17 is a sequential passage, whereas ritornello c (mm. 23–30) is clearly cadential, although the registral skips in the upper strings provide motivic contrast and heighten the tension in the drive toward the D-minor cadence in measure 30.

Diagram of Opening Ritornello

RITORNELLO a	EXTENSION	RITORNELLO b	RITORNELLO c
mm. 1–7	mm. 8–16	mm. 17–22	mm. 23–30
i–III	III	III	V–i (cadential)

Vivaldi's highly idiomatic treatment of both the viola d'amore and the lute is equally unconventional. Throughout the concerto, he takes advantage of their ability to play double stops and virtuosic running passages, as well as having them double the violins and basso continuo respectively in the tutti sections. Sometimes he treats the two instruments imitatively in a manner that underscores their contrasting sonorities; at other times he ramps up the intensity by having them play together, as in measures 135–52, the climactic final solo section in the Allegro. As shown in the second diagram, Vivaldi omits the viola and continuo in all the solo sections. On the surface this orchestration has a practical component, as it allows the quiet instruments to be clearly audible. (Vivaldi guarantees they will be heard, too, by indicating that the upper strings should use mutes to dampen the sound.) But by allowing other instruments (in this instance the violins) to take on the role of the basso continuo—a technique known as "bassetto" or little bass—Vivaldi gives the music a light, effervescent quality and calls attention to the viola d'amore's luminous timbre. The absence of the basso continuo also creates dramatic interest throughout the concerto, as the lute and viola d'amore compete for primacy as soloists, while the violins—who typically take the lead—are often forced to take on the continuo's role as harmonic foundation.

Diagram of Movement 1

FORM	A	B	A'	C	A"	C	A
RITORNELLO SECTION	a-*ext*-bc	Solo	a'bc	Solo	a'c	Solo	a-*ext*-bc
MEASURES	mm. 1–30	mm. 31–53	mm. 53–69	mm. 69–94	mm. 94–106	mm. 106–52	mm. 153–82
KEY	i . . . i	i–III	III	III . . . v	V . . . i	i . . . i	i . . . i
CONTINUO INSTRUMENTS	viola and continuo (including solo lute)	first and second violins	viola and continuo	first and second violins	viola and continuo	first and second violins	viola and continuo

16

BARBARA STROZZI (1619–1677)

Cantate, ariete a una, due, e tre voci: Op. 3: Begli occhi
Vocal duet, published 1654

"Begli occhi" by Barbara Strozzi is published in *Barbara Strozzi: Cantate, ariete a una, due, e tre voci*, Opus 3, edited by Gail Archer, Recent Researches in the Music of the Baroque Era, vol. 83. Middleton, WI: A-R Editions, Inc., 1997. Used with permission. All rights reserved.

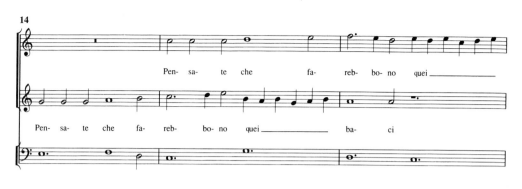

Pen- sa- te che fa- reb- bo- no quei _____

Pen- sa- te che fa- reb- bo- no quei _____ ba- ci

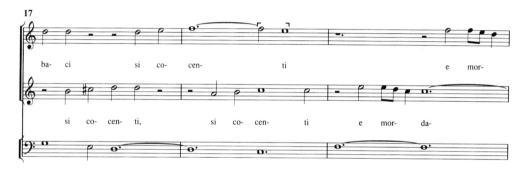

ba- ci si co- cen- ti e mor-

si co- cen- ti, si co- cen- ti e mor- da-

-da- ci; Lan- gue l'a- ni- ma,

- ci; _____ Lan- gue l'a- ni- ma, lan- gue,

lan- gue, e il _____ cor vien _____ me- no, e il _____ cor vien _____

e il _____ cor, e il _____ cor vien _____ me- no, e il _____ cor vien _____

Mi ferite, oh begli occhi.	*You wound me, O beautiful eyes.*
Pensate che farebbono quei baci	*Think what these kisses could do,*
si concenti e mordaci.	*so burning and biting.*
Langue l'anima, langue, e il cor	*My soul languishes and my heart wavers.*
vien meno.	
Ahi, ch'io vi moro in seno.	*Ah, that I die for you in my breast.*
Pensate che farebbono gli strali	*Think what these arrows could do,*
si pungenti e mortali.	*so pointed and deadly.*
Langue l'anima, langue, e il cor	*My soul languishes and my heart wavers.*
vien meno.	
Ahi, ch'io vi moro in seno.	*Ah, that I die for you in my breast.*
Ma forse non morrò senza vendetta	*But perhaps I will not die without revenge,*
ch'al fin chi morte da la morte aspetta.	*for he who gives death must wait for it*
	in the end.

Barbara Strozzi is a unique figure in seventeenth-century music. As the author of eight printed volumes of vocal chamber music (one of which is no longer extant), she was among her generation's most prolific composers of cantatas and arias. Unlike the composer and singer Francesca Caccini, who was employed by the Medici, Strozzi neither served a single patron nor owed allegiance to any court, although many of her works are dedicated to nobles (and she may have had a liaison with the duke of Mantua). Instead, the adopted daughter of Giulio Strozzi—well known in Venice for his poetry and librettos, which were set by Monteverdi and others—came of age in the rarefied world of the Venetian academies, where her gender was both a liability and an asset.

As a singer who performed for the Accademia degli Unisoni (Academy of the Sonorous Ones), a subset of the Incogniti (Unknown Ones)—the Venetian academy that had served as a magnet for the most "libertine" writers on the Italian peninsula—Strozzi was certainly an object of desire and fascination. She must also have been accustomed to the underlying anti-female message in many of their writings, some of which were directed toward her. As a gifted composer, however, she was in the rare position of providing musical settings for many of the texts that dwelled on female beauty and sexuality. While the majority of the love poems we have considered previously in this anthology have been presented from a male perspective, many of Strozzi's settings provide insights into the female point of view, regardless of whether the poet is speaking from a male, female, or gender-neutral position.

"Begli occhi" is from Strozzi's *Cantate, ariete* (Cantatas, Ariettas), Op. 3, of 1654, a collection of short arias and multisectioned works that she called cantatas. It focuses on the familiar conceit of death as a metaphor for sexual pleasure. It features two sopranos, whose intertwining voices musically enact the intimate physical experience described in the text. The poem is structured in a somewhat idiosyncratic way, which may suggest Strozzi's hand in its crafting, so that it might better suit her musical setting. The initial 7-syllable line stands apart from the rest, followed by two four-line strophes comprised of 7- and 11-syllable lines (compare Giulio Caccini's setting of "Dovrò dunque morire," Anthology 2), in which the lover asks the beloved to imagine the burning and biting of kisses and the piercing arrows of love, both of which make the poet languish and die within. The final pair of endecasyllabic (11-syllable) lines contains an ironic twist: the poet will have his revenge, since the lover who provides sexual fulfillment for his or her partner must wait that much longer for pleasure.

Strozzi's musical setting calls attention to the erotic nature of the poetry, using many of the strategies found in her other vocal works: lengthy melismas, frequent shifts between duple and triple meter, unexpected dissonances, and abrupt changes in vocal style and texture that sensitively correspond to the poetic sentiments. The setting of the opening line, for instance, creates a vivid aural impression of the increasing excitement of an encounter between two lovers. The two sopranos sing together in half and quarter notes and with a single voice crossing; the note values then accelerate as the eighth-note imitative passage that begins in measure 3 is first varied and then broken apart into an exchange of wordless sixteenth-note sighs on the exclamation "oh" (mm. 6–8). It is almost as if the wounding eyes have temporarily left the poet speechless.

In the two subsequent strophes, Strozzi shifts to a lighthearted triple-meter aria style in diatonic C major as she imagines how dangerous lovemaking could be. The biting kisses of the first strophe, marked with a dissonance on the second beat of measure 19, are differentiated from the sharp arrows of the second strophe, rendered with a passage of emphatic descending quarter notes outlining a C-major triad in imitative counterpoint (mm. 45–48). Such painful pleasure leads to languor, made explicit not only with a return to duple meter but with a chromatic ascent through G♯ and C♯ (mm. 21–23 and 49–51), while the breathless wavering of the heart is underscored by shifts between homophony and imitation, as well as unexpected rests. Strozzi further avoids regularity by varying the musical settings of repeated poetic fragments, such as the phrase "ch'io vi moro."

Changes in meter underscore the irony of the poem's last two lines. The shift between 3 (notated in the accompanying score as $^6_2$) and $^3_2$ (m. 74) creates what is essentially a suddenly slower tempo that emphasizes the line "ch'al fin chi morte da la morte aspetta" (for he who gives death must wait for it in the end). The repetition of the line, however, is interrupted by a subsequent shift to duple meter (m. 92) that isolates the word "aspetta." As the two lovers

anticipate the climax, the voices playfully interact: the second soprano introduces a melisma to which the first responds (m. 93) and, after a brief exchange
(mm. 94–95), they join together, suspended on the dominant as they prepare
for the final cadence.

Strozzi's setting of the poem is suggestive from a number of perspectives.
The duet is not only about lovemaking; its dynamic structure—the alternation
between diatonic aria style and more dissonant, languid recitation—actually
imitates the pace of an erotic encounter from excitement to fulfillment. The
use of two equal voices, with frequent crossings and exchanges of motives,
seems an apt way of underscoring the poem's underlying message about mutual
satisfaction in lovemaking. Finally, although the poet avoids any reference to
the gender of the protagonist, we might well imagine that the duet represents
Strozzi's own view of sensual pleasure.

17

ARCANGELO CORELLI (1653–1713)

Violin Sonata in A Major, Op. 5, No. 9
Violin sonata, published 1700

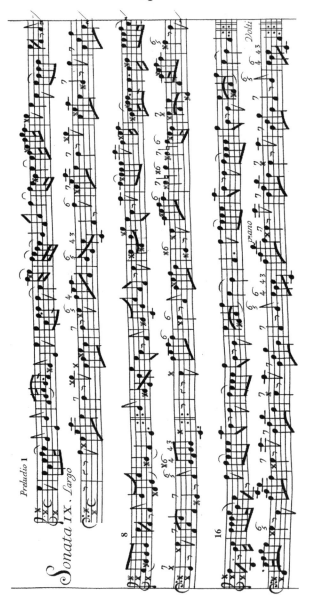

From Arcangelo Corelli, *Sonata e violino e violone e cimbalo, opera quinta.* [Rome]: G. Pietra Santa, [1700].
Pages 138–42: Rare Books and Special Collections, Princeton University Library.

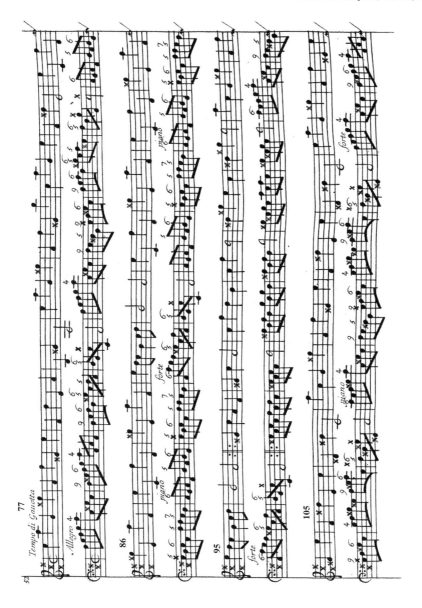

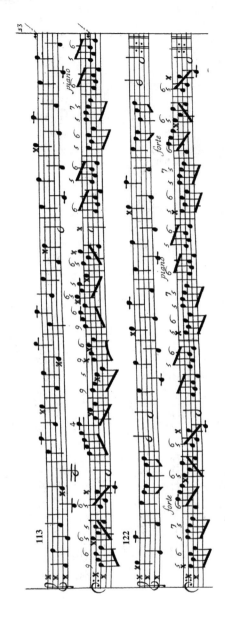

Arcangelo Corelli's beautifully engraved edition of the Op. 5 sonatas for violin and continuo would assume the same importance for violinists as Caccini's *Le nuove musiche* (see Anthology 2) had for singers nearly 100 years previously. The 12 sonatas of the set were probably composed over a period of decades prior to their publication—according to the British music historian Charles Burney, Corelli spent years revising them before they were sent to press. Nevertheless, the Op. 5 sonatas became what we might describe as "instant classics." Young violinists flocked to Rome to study with the master. The sonatas remained a central part of the violin repertory over the next century, with more than 50 reprintings on the Italian peninsula, in France, and especially in Amsterdam and London, where Corelli's music created a seemingly inexhaustible demands for Italian players and violin music.

All of this may seem something of a mystery to the modern listener, for whom Corelli's sonatas, as lovely as they are, epitomize "typical" Baroque music. Indeed, the relative simplicity of these works is a hallmark of Corelli's style. The printed versions from 1700 are not technically demanding and do not require, for instance, the violinist to play in unusually high positions. Corelli's tendency to favor sequences in which the bass moves by fourth or fifth may also sound conventional to modern ears. What appealed to contemporary listeners, however, was the purity and clarity of Corelli's writing: his preference for the dominant and the relative major; his judicious use of dissonance; and the rhythmic drive and forward motion that made cadences so satisfying.

The lyrical Preludio of the A-Major Sonata is in the style of an allemande, with its slow duple meter, binary form, and characteristic upbeat. Corelli uses the marking Largo (slow), which gives the violinist considerable license to ornament the apparently simple melodic line. That simplicity, however, belies the intricate structure of the movement. The violin's range is indeed relatively restricted—a bit more than two octaves between low A and high C♯—and most of the melody is confined to a single octave in the middle register. However, the initial four-bar phrase demonstrates the care with which Corelli coordinates melody and harmony. The symmetry of the motion from I to V and V/V to V in measures 1 and 2 is mirrored by the violin's melody: each measure begins with an ornamented turn figure hovering around C♯ and is followed by a downward skip to E. This strong articulation of the dominant is followed by a powerful thrust toward the tonic cadence in measure 4. As the violin jumps an octave from E to E and climbs into the upper register for the bold sixteenth-note descent from the high A, Corelli quickens the harmonic rhythm in measure 3 while also increasing the tension with the seventh on beat 1 and a 4–3 suspension on beat 3. Some of the movement's poignancy comes from Corelli's use of a repeated-note sigh figure, first hinted at on beats 2 and 3 in measure 3.

It becomes an important motive on beats 3 and 4 in measure 6 and is used throughout the movement, often in sequences of expressive 7–6 suspensions. Corelli uses this technique to particular effect in the final seven measures of the Preludio, where the plaintive character is underscored by a shift of dynamics to *piano*, creating an echo effect.

The second movement is a standard Italian gigue that begins with an upbeat in compound meter ($\frac{12}{8}$) and a fast tempo (Allegro). The cheerful quality of the Giga is heightened by the playful exchanges between violin and continuo, as in measures 38–40, where the violin, in its lower register, adds a sequential commentary to the triplets in the continuo. The sequential passage that opens the **B** section in the dominant gives way to a return to the tonic in the middle of measure 51 and a literal repeat of the first 12 measures of the **A** section, continuing to a different ending. In measures 63–65, the continuo traces a stepwise-descending A-major scale, alternating root-position and first-inversion chords, while the violin settles into its lower register; Corelli once again inserts an echo, repeating these three measures *piano*. This leads to a brief Adagio in F♯ minor, in which the soaring violin is supported by a chromatically descending bass that leads to a half cadence on C♯. In the final Tempo di Gavotta, Corelli establishes a distinctive, almost rustic character by contrasting the four-square violin melody, with its steady quarter notes and large skips, with the basso continuo's unbroken eighth notes in mainly stepwise motion. (See Anthology 18 for an example of a gavotte in the French style by François Couperin.)

Although Corelli's score printed in Rome in 1700 (reproduced here in facsimile) contains relatively few ornaments, highly decorated versions of this and the other Op. 5 sonatas are found in numerous printed and manuscript sources. The level of complexity seems to have increased throughout the eighteenth century, as each generation tried to outdo the previous one. What kinds of ornaments, and how many, Corelli himself might have preferred remains an open question. The 1710 Amsterdam edition of the first six sonatas features richly embellished Adagios purporting to be "as Corelli played them." (Scholars now believe that this may well be the case.) The survival of so many ornamented versions indicates that eighteenth-century players would have considered an unadorned performance of these works as incomplete.

18

FRANÇOIS COUPERIN (1668–1733)

Pièces de clavecin: Order 3, *La ténébreuse*, and Order 6, *Les moissonneurs*

Harpsichord pieces, published 1713 and 1716–17, respectively

La Ténébreuse

Allemande

From *Oeuvres Complètes de François Couperin*, Vol. 2, *Pièces de Clavecin*, Part 1, Publiées par Maurice Cauchie et revues d'après les sources par Kenneth Gilbert (Monaco: L'Oiseau-Lyre, 1980). Reprinted by permission; and *Oeuvres Complètes de François Couperin*, Vol. 2, *Pièces de Clavecin*, Part 2, Publiées par Maurice Cauchie et revues d'après les sources par Kenneth Gilbert (Monaco: L'Oiseau-Lyre, 1980). Reprinted by permission.

Les Moissonneurs

Rondeau.

Gayement.

1er Couplet.

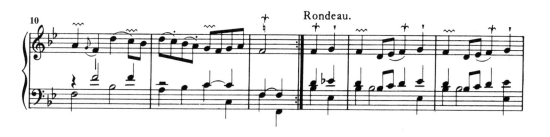

Rondeau.

In 1713, while François Couperin was still providing music to entertain Louis XIV, his family, and courtiers at Versailles, he published the first of his four books of *Pièces de clavecin* (Harpsichord Pieces). These four volumes consist of 27 *ordres*, or suites, and encompass a variety of subgenres: standard French dance movements, descriptive character pieces, movements dedicated to various individuals, and hybrids of one or more of these categories.

Both *La ténébreuse* and *Les moissonneurs* belong to two categories: the descriptive and the dance. *La ténébreuse*, the first movement of the third *ordre*, with its binary form, duple meter, and short one-note upbeat, is clearly recognizable as an allemande. As with many of his harpsichord pieces, however, the title conveys several additional layers of meaning. The word *ténèbre* refers to darkness or sadness, and Couperin achieves this by exploiting the rich, dark sonorities of the lowest register of the harpsichord. The key of C minor, associated with *tombeaux* and other memorial works, confirms this melancholy feeling. In light of Louis's increasing piety in the years following his marriage to Madame de Maintenon, the title may also refer to the Tenebrae service, part of the Holy Week liturgy during which the candles in church are slowly extinguished. Couperin wrote a set of *Leçons de ténèbres* (Tenebrae Lessons) to be performed at this solemn service.

It is not surprising that Couperin's allemande shares some surface features with the Lamento that begins Froberger's Suite in C Major (see Anthology 8). Froberger was known to François's uncle, Louis Couperin, who modeled one of his unmeasured preludes on a toccata by the German composer (see Fig. 4.5 in *Music in the Baroque*). These two allemandes by Froberger and Couperin share many common traits: They are both in binary form, have a melancholy affect, use *style brisé* extensively, and speak in short phrases unlike the flowing allemande that opens Corelli's A-Major Sonata (see Anthology 17). With its moderate tempo and majestic dotted rhythms, Couperin's *La ténébreuse* would also have reminded his listeners of the French overture (a stately movement in ternary form that Jean-Baptiste Lully and other composers used so often at the beginning of operas, oratorios, and other dramatic works to convey a sense of regal splendor).

La ténébreuse is an excellent example of Couperin's meticulous notation of note values, articulations, and *agréments* (ornaments). The latter are not optional or open to interpretation, but must be performed exactly as prescribed in the ornament tables that Couperin and his contemporaries so often supplied for their collections of keyboard music. In the first measure, observe the careful notation of the mordents (which Couperin calls *pincés*) on beats 2, 3, and 4 of the left hand, and the double-stem on the G of beat 4, indicating that the player *must* hold that note for the entire beat. In the right-hand part of the same measure, Couperin evokes the "overdotting" characteristic of the French overture by subdividing the second half of beat 2 (note the double-stem again) as three sixty-fourth notes. This is incorrect mathematically but indicates that the figure can be played as late and as freely as good taste (*bon goût*) allows. The right hand also features appoggiaturas, or *ports de voix* (literally, carryings of the voice), on beats 3 and 4; these were performed in a variety of rhythms that reflect the natural inflections of the French language.

In the **B** section, Couperin relinquishes the somber French overture and creates a plaintive, almost sighing affect in measure 11 with melodic thirds slurred in pairs, called *coulés* (from the verb *couler,* meaning to run or flow). This notation tells the player to sustain the first note while playing the second, which is then held somewhat shorter than notated; the double-stemming on the first note of each pair reinforces the message. Another ornament symbol appears on the second, third, and fourth eighth notes of the right hand in measure 12: the *arpègement* (arpeggio), in which the player rolls the chords from bottom to top, adding to the sense of drama and intensity. Couperin returns to a darker affect in the second half of the **B** section, beginning in measure 16, where the sixteenth-note rests ensure that the offbeat tenor voice is played crisply, further highlighting the starkness of the repeated chords.

The affect, style, form, and approach to the harpsichord could not be more different in *Les moissonneurs* (The Reapers), the initial movement of Couperin's sixth *ordre. Les moissonneurs* is also a dance—a gavotte, similar to the one we encountered in Corelli's violin sonata (see Anthology 17). The gavotte is usually in a moderate tempo, often in cut time, and in duple meter with an upbeat comprised of two quarter notes. (Corelli dispenses with the preparatory upbeat figure in his Tempo di Gavotta, a sign that the dance was intended for the ears rather than the feet.) The gavotte is the ideal dance type to represent the rhythmic motion of reapers harvesting wheat in the field with their scythes. Couperin reinforces the allusion to cutting by placing an *aspiration* (a sign resembling a modern accent mark that tells the performer to play the note quite short and sharply) on the second note of the upbeat figures.

In this movement, Couperin uses rondo rather than binary form. Rondo form features a usually simple refrain (*rondeau* in French)—in this case, a repetitive melody that hovers around the fifth degree of the scale (mm. 1–8)—which is heard in alternation with a series of episodes called *couplets,* of which there are three in *Les moissonneurs.* Though enlivened with *agréments,* the homophonic *rondeau* theme and *couplets* are almost completely lacking in dissonances or rhythmic complexities. Indeed, the third *couplet,* which begins with a variation of the *rondeau* theme up an octave, captures something of the innocence and sweetness typical of the pastoral make-believe that was all the rage in the most exclusive Parisian circles in the eighteenth century.

19

JEAN-PHILIPPE RAMEAU (1683–1764)

Platée, Act 2, scene 3: *A l'aspect de ce nuage*
Opera, 1745

The lower part of the cloud separates and moves upward.
Jupiter appears in the form of a donkey; a small cupid drapes him in garlands of flowers.

The birds make a great racket when they notice the owl, which, after perching for a while, flies away without Plataea noticing.

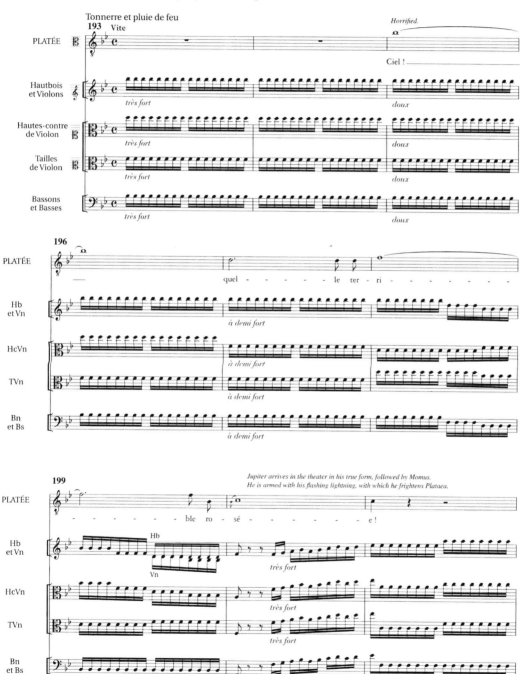

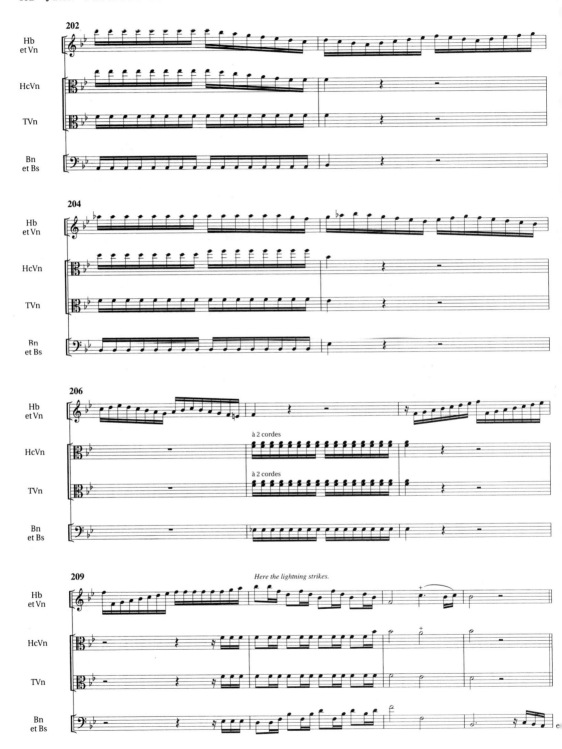

1. AIR

A l'aspect de ce nuage,	*From the look of this cloud,*
je ne saurois m'abuser,	*I know not to be deceived,*
Jupiter sait tout oser:	*Jupiter knows to dare all:*
Mais aurai-je le courage	*But do I have the courage*
de recevoir son hommage	*to receive his homage*
ou de le refuser?	*or to refuse it?*
Le nuage s'entr'ouvre,	*The cloud is opening up,*
je vois du mouvement:	*I see something move:*
je crois qu'il me découvre,	*I believe that it will reveal to me*
mon adorable amant.	*my charming suitor.*

2. ACCOMPANIED RECITATIVE

Quelle métamorphose!	*What a metamorphosis!*
Dois-je approcher? Je n'ose.	*Should I come near? I do not dare.*

3. ACCOMPANIED AIR

C'est une épreuve assurément	*This is surely a test*
que Jupiter prépare à ma flamme nouvelle.	*that Jupiter has prepared of my new passion.*
Venez, venez, j'y suis fidelle,	*Come, come, I am faithful,*
quel que soit ce déguisement.	*regardless of the disguise.*
Apprenez-moi ce qu'amour vous inspire,	*Teach me what inspires love in you,*
et ce que votre coeur prétend.	*and what your heart desires.*
Vous soupirez et je soupire;	*You sigh and I sigh;*
il suffit d'un si doux accent;	*a sweet accent is all that is necessary;*
vous dites tout, sans me rien dire.	*you say all without saying anything.*
Ah! Que l'amour est éloquent!	*Ah! How eloquent is love!*
Quoi! Vous disparoissez!	*What? You disappear!*
Sous quel nouveau plumage	*Under what new plumage*
me représentez-vous	*are you presenting yourself to me*
le plus beau des hiboux?	*as the most beautiful of owls?*
Oiseaux de ce bocage,	*Birds of this grove,*
venez tous, chantez.	*come here, all of you, sing.*
Quel cris! Quel ramage!	*What cries! What racket!*
Oiseaux, vous en êtes jaloux,	*Birds, you are jealous of him,*
changez de language,	*change your speech,*

4. AIR

rendez homage
au plus beau des hiboux.

give homage
to the most beautiful of owls.

5. ACCOMPANIED RECITATIVE

Hélas! Il s'envole?
Je ne le vois plus.
Jupiter, Jupiter . . . mes cris
sont superflus.
Il faudra donc que mon
coeur s'en désole.
Hélas! Il s'envole!
Je ne le vois plus.
Ciel! Quelle terrible rosée!

Alas, he has flown away?
I don't see him any more.
Jupiter . . . Jupiter . . . my cries mean nothing.

It thus must be that my heart is sad.

Alas! He has flown away.
I don't see him any more.
Heavens! What horrible dew!

Jean-Philippe Rameau's *Platée*, to a libretto by Adrien Joseph Le Valois d'Orville, after a play by Jacques Autreau, was first presented on March 31, 1745, as the conclusion of a month-long celebration for the wedding of the French dauphin and the Infanta Maria Theresa. The story concerns the goddess Juno's jealousy over her husband Jupiter's many infidelities. Since their bickering has caused bad weather on earth, the king of the mountain, Citheron, comes up with a scheme to trick Juno: Jupiter is to propose marriage to an ugly swamp creature named Plataea (Platée, played by the tenor Pierre de Jélyotte cross-dressed as a female water nymph). Plataea is sufficiently ignorant of her own unattractiveness to imagine that Jupiter would indeed desire her. The final scene of the opera opens with a mock marriage ceremony. Just as Jupiter is about to speak his vows, Juno enters, removes Plataea's veil, and realizes that she has been tricked, whereupon the two immortals make up their quarrel and ascend to Olympus.

In Act 2, scene 3, Plataea has her first encounter with Jupiter. Rameau's music traces the nymph's responses as the god descends from the heavens with the god Momus, in a cloud, transforming himself first into a donkey and then an owl—before resuming his own guise. The frequent shifts between air and recitative, with vigorous participation from the orchestra and shifts in tempo and affect brilliantly capture Plataea's changing emotions: her unwarranted pride in her own beauty, her desire for Jupiter, and her surprise and fear at his various metamorphoses.

Rameau is particularly successful at creating for Plataea an exaggerated rhetorical style that becomes quite comic when considered in the context of her self-aggrandizement. Observe, for instance, the way in which the phrase "adorable amant" (charming suitor) is expanded with an elaborate melisma in measures 51–55, including the sustained high C in measures 51–52; the Italianate runs on the verb "chantez" (sing) in measures 132–33; and the melodramatic expansion, with gasps and a climactic florid passage in measures 186–90, on "s'envole," when Jupiter flies away.

At other times Rameau exaggerates the nymph's feminine qualities, as in the air "C'est une épreuve assurément" (This is surely a test), beginning in measure 64. Here he specifically directs the singer and players not to employ *notes inégales* (the unwritten practice of altering the rhythm so that passages notated as equal are performed with alternating long and short values): the eighth notes played equally might well have been intended to imitate the delicate steps of the cross-dressed water nymph.

The humor is further enhanced by Rameau's skillful orchestral writing. Note particularly the way the orchestra interacts with Plataea, sometimes taking on the role of the otherwise silent Jupiter. (The orchestra plays an equally prominent role in Lully's *Armide*; see Anthology 13.) In the first air, "A l'aspect de ce nuage" (From the look of this cloud), the duet between the violin and the voice (especially in mm. 23–32) evokes the swamp creature's imagined encounter with Jupiter. In measures 89–97, the orchestra mockingly echoes Plataea's sighs, creating animalistic sounds appropriate for the donkey whose form Jupiter has temporarily assumed. In order to represent the high-pitched clamor of the birds after they glimpse Jove in the guise of an owl, Rameau uses the flageolets (a small recorder-like instrument sometimes used to imitate bird calls), playing insistent triplet figures, along with first and second violins playing frenetic sixteenth notes (mm. 134–138). The orchestra's boldest interjection begins in measure 193, as the frenetic sixteenth notes reiterating the tonic and dominant in B♭ major invoke a familiar convention from French opera and cantata: storm music, portraying the clap of thunder associated with Jupiter. By the time Plataea actually meets Jupiter in human form at the conclusion of the scene, it is not surprising that she is too awestruck even to speak.

20

DIETERICH BUXTEHUDE (CA. 1637–1707)

Membra Jesu nostri, BuxWV 75: *Ad cor:*
Vulnerasti cor meum

Cantata, ca. 1680

1. Sonata

2. Concerto

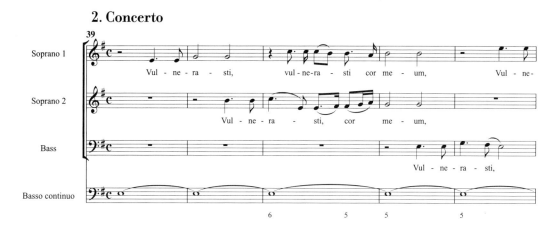

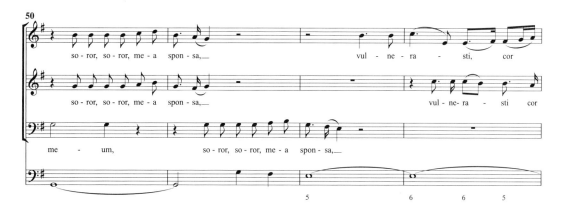

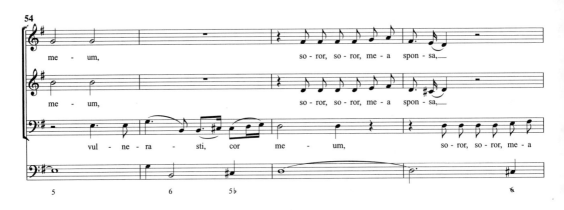

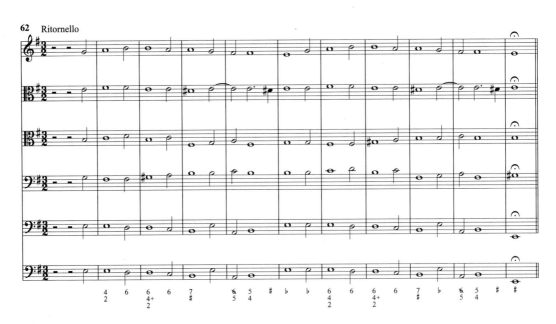

4. Aria

Soprano 2

Per me - dul - lam cor dis me - i, pec - ca - to - ris at - que re - i tu - us a - mor trans - fe-

Basso continuo

ra - tur, quo cor tu - um ra - pi - a - tur   tu - us a - mor trans - fe - ra - tur, quo cor

tu - um ra - pi - a - tur lan - - - guens a - mo - ris vul - ne - re, lan - guens a - mo - ris vul - ne-

Ritornello

re,

5. Aria

6. Concerto

2. CONCERTO (SOPRANOS 1 AND 2 AND BASS)

Vulnerasti cor meum,	*You have wounded my heart,*
soror mea, sponsa,	*my sister, my bride,*
vulnerasti cor meum.	*you have wounded my heart.*

3. ARIA (SOPRANO 1)

Summi regis cor, aveto,	*Heart of the highest king, I greet you,*
te saluto corde laeto,	*I salute you with a joyous heart,*
te complecti me delectat	*it delights me to embrace you*
et hoc meum cor affectat,	*and my heart aspires to this:*
ut ad te loquar, animes.	*that you move me to speak to you.*

4. ARIA (SOPRANO 2)

Per medullam cordis mei,	*Through the marrow of my heart,*
peccatoris atque rei,	*of a sinner and culprit,*
tuus amor transferatur,	*may your love be conveyed*
quo cor tuum rapiatur	*by whom your heart was seized,*
languens amoris vulnere.	*languishing through the wound of love.*

5. ARIA (BASS WITH VIOL ENSEMBLE)

Viva cordis voce clamo,	*I call with the living voice of the heart,*
dulce cor, te namque amo,	*sweet heart, for I love you,*
ad cor meum inclinare,	*to incline to my heart,*
ut se possit applicare	*so that it may draw close*
devoto tibi pectore.	*to you with devoted breast.*

6. CONCERTO (SOPRANOS 1 AND 2, BASS, AND VIOL ENSEMBLE)

Vulnerasti cor meum, etc.	*You have wounded my heart, etc.*

During his four decades as organist at St. Mary's Church in Lübeck, Dieterich Buxtehude composed a substantial number of vocal works. Outstanding among them is a set of seven Latin cantatas entitled *Membra Jesu nostri* (The Limbs of Our Jesus), which survive in a manuscript dedicated in 1680 to Buxtehude's friend, the organist Gustav Düben. The texts for this cycle are drawn from a medieval poem attributed to Arnulf of Louvain, *Salve mundi salutare* (Long Live the Salvation of the World), focusing on the suffering of Christ. Each stanza is devoted to the seven wounds of Christ's body: the feet, the knees, the hands, the side, the breast, the heart, and the face, which in turn were used as the central texts for the seven cantatas. Buxtehude begins each cantata with a meditative instrumental sonata followed by a sacred concerto—a setting of a biblical text with a thematic link to the poem (this is usually reprised at the end). Instrumental ritornelli are placed between the movements.

It is not surprising that Buxtehude chose to begin and end the sixth cantata, addressed to the heart (*ad cor*), with an excerpt from the *Song of Songs*, which inspired so many seventeenth-century composers. The image of the wounded heart from the Old Testament helps listeners contemplate the joyful heart of the faithful Christian and the mixture of love and sorrow that Lutherans associated with Christ's wounds. Buxtehude's cantata captures these seemingly antithetical affects with extraordinary depth. The opening instrumental sonata is remarkable for its unusual scoring: an ensemble of five viols lends the work a somber, mystical tone. The contrast between joy and sorrow is aptly captured in the alternation between majestic homophonic Adagio passages marked by quarter- and half-note movement (the second and third of these are in triple meter) and imitative Allegro sections with exhuberant dotted rhythms.

In the first concerto (no. 2) for two soprano voices, singing in imitation and in parallel thirds above the bass, Buxtehude combines gestures associated with expressions of love with the sorrowful affect depicted in the yearning ascending minor thirds and the impassioned minor-sixth descents from the upper register of each voice (m. 41 in soprano 2, m. 44 in soprano 1, and m. 49 in the bass). Buxtehude uses a lighter affect for the two soprano arias (nos. 3 and 4) and associated ritornelli. Dotted rhythms, symmetrical phrases, and ascending vocal lines encapsulate the joyful tone of the first soprano's aria, in which the heart of Christ is greeted. He employs the same music for "Per medullum cordi mei," the second soprano's aria, adding an expressive melisma on the word "languens" (languishing) in measures 92–93. The drama is enhanced in the bass aria (no. 5) as the viols join in imitative dialogue with the voice, as the theology of love transcends the sorrow of Christ's death.

In the final movement, what might have been a mere repetition of the opening concerto is utterly transformed by the addition of the viols, which create a novel instrumental halo around the voices. One of Buxtehude's most ingenious moves is to take the eighth-note motive used for the second half of the verse "soror mea, sponsa," (my sister, my bride) and give it to the viols, indicating (with phrase markings) that it should be played with a tremolo. A comparison of measures 58–61 in movement no. 2 with its corresponding portion in movement no. 6 (mm. 139–142) shows how the skillful integration of the viols not only enriches the texture but heightens the emotional response. The viols also provide an eloquent conclusion by echoing the final *piano* statement of the most important phrase: "cor, cor meum" (my heart), testifying to the love symbolized by Christ's wounds.

Ouverture burlesque de Quixotte, TWV 55: G10

Overture-suite, ca. 1725–30

[1] Ouverture

From Georg Philipp Telemann, *Ouverture burlesque de Quixotte,* TWV 55: G10. Edition by Brian Clark. Reprinted by permission.

[2] The Awakening of Don Quixote

[3] His attack on the windmills

[4] His sighs of love after Princess Dulcinea

[5] Sancho Panza mocked

[6a] The Gallop of Rocinante.

[Fine]

[6b] That [the gallop] of Sancho Panza's mule

Da Capo The Gallop

[7] Don Quixote at rest

[Fine]

Violin 1

doux

Violin 2 & Viola

doux

Da Capo

The overture-suite may have been an essentially Germanic phenomenon, but it was largely inspired by the northern European fascination with French music, including the sets of instrumental music from Lully's operas published by Amsterdam music printers such as Estienne Roger. In response, German composers, especially those who had trained in France with Lully, compiled "overture-suites" from printed scores of French operas; they became so popular that German musicians began composing entirely original overture-suites. These were usually written for four- or five-part string ensemble and included a broad selection of movements, many either implicitly or overtly programmatic. They thus retained some of the theatrical flavor of their French cousins, while exploiting orchestral resources in novel ways.

The genre caught the imagination of Georg Philipp Telemann, who began composing overture-suites while still a student at the University of Leipzig. They were particularly well suited to the interests and abilities of players in the various collegia musica that he directed, and were also appropriate for use at the courts with which Telemann was associated. By 1718 Telemann claimed to have written over 200 overture-suites; 125 survive, though only 10 were published during his lifetime—a surprisingly low proportion given Telemann's interest in marketing and publishing his own works.

Telemann's overture-suites are remarkably varied. While some are scored for strings only, others incorporate winds or brass, and still others feature one or more solo instruments, much like concertos. Telemann's overture-suites show his characteristic delight in using various national styles—French, Italian, German, and Polish—to create a kind of international voice that appealed to cosmopolitan consumers of music in north German cities such as Hamburg, where he spent a substantial part of his career.

Telemann's *Ouverture burlesque de Quixotte* (Burlesque Overture of Quixote) is among his most evocative overture-suites, capturing in music much of the satirical tone of Miguel de Cervantes's *Don Quixote*. Among the many eighteenth-century operas inspired by the 1605 novel was Francesco Conti's *Don Chischiotte in Sierra Morena*, first produced in Vienna in 1719 and reprised in Hamburg in 1722, a performance that Telemann may well have attended. Telemann himself would go on to write an opera based on *Don Quixote* in 1761.

The *Ouverture burlesque* contains seven movements in binary form, the last six of which were given titles that refer to specific episodes in the novel:

1. Overture
2. The Awakening of Don Quixote
3. His Attack on the Windmills
4. His Sighs of Love after Princess Dulcinea
5. Sancho Panza Mocked

6a. The Gallop of Rocinante and (6b) that of Sancho Panza's Mule

7. Don Quixote at Rest

A gentle mocking tone pervades the entire work. While the French over-ture (No. 1) that opens the *Ouverture burlesque* would seem to be exempt, since Telemann provides no programmatic label, the comic contrasts in the abrupt juxtapositions of rhythmic and thematic ideas suggest otherwise. Instead of the noble chords with dotted rhythms that are associated with the entrance of the monarch in the French opera, the strings seem to saunter lazily into the lower register (m. 4). The grace notes in the first violins in measures 6 and 8 erase any pretensions of grandeur and majesty. The unexpected flurry of descending thirty-second-note scales and repeating-note figures in measures 10 and 12 are nothing less than the aural equivalent of slipping on a banana peel. Even the contrapuntal second section starting at measure 23, with its swirling sixteenth notes, provides more than a hint of the antics to come, particularly when the orchestra plays in unison, as in measures 67–73.

The second movement, which depicts the awakening of the hero, is notable for its harmonic stasis: nearly the entire **A** section of the binary form plays out over a G pedal. (Perhaps the hero is having trouble getting out of bed). Comedy returns in full force in the third movement, as Don Quixote mounts a chaotic and ineffective attack on the windmills (which he mistakes for giant combat-ants). Fragmented pairs of descending eighth notes signal the charge, whirring sixteenth notes mimic the motion of the windmills, and *stile concitato* evokes the excitement of battle. The fourth movement, representing the hero's sighs of love for the unattainable Dulcinea, opens with a prominent unprepared 4–3 suspen-sion that will reappear throughout the movement. Telemann even sets up a dia-logue of sigh figures: the initial eighth-note sighs are answered by mini-sobs at the level of the sixteenth note. The rhythmic contrasts in the fifth movement provide an apt representation of Sancho Panza, Don Quixote's faithful squire. Note, for instance, how Telemann interrupts what would have otherwise been a quite conventional 8-bar phrase **A** section, slowing down the harmonic rhythm in measures 2–3 with the octave Gs decorated with thirty-second notes, as if to mock the squire's clumsy gait. The effect is even more striking in the **B** section (mm. 12–13), when the same passage is heard in E minor.

Two of the novel's most colorful characters, Don Quixote's horse, Rocinante, and Sancho Panza's mule, are the subjects of the sixth movement, which comprises two sections, each in binary form, to be performed **ABA**. Rocinante's elegant and steady gallop is featured in No. 6a; she lands nimbly on the downbeat of each mea-sure. The mule, on the other hand (No. 6b), is far less precise or consistent in his attempt to keep up with the tempo; note, for instance, the offbeat sixteenth-note runs in the **B** section. The concluding "Don Quixote at Rest" (No. 7), a rounded binary, is a marvelous, tongue-in-cheek depiction of the crazy knight whose mind was probably never at rest. The G pedal in the bass with the shifting tonic and dominant harmonies above gives the impression of a peasant playing bagpipes, adding to the pastoral flavor.

Mystery Sonatas: *Crucifixion* Sonata (No. 10)

Sonata for violin and continuo, ca. 1676

Facsimile of manuscript with engraving

From Heinrich Ignaz Franz Biber, *Mystery* Sonatas: Crucifixion Sonata (No. 10). Page 195: Bayerische Staatsbibliothek. The score proper begins on page 196.

Praeludium.

The set of violin sonatas by Heinrich Ignaz Franz Biber referred to as the *Mystery* or *Rosary* Sonatas are among the most unusual in the repertory. They survive in a single, beautifully copied manuscript (see the facsimile on p. 195), currently held at the Bavarian State Library in Munich. Since the title page is lost, scholars have drawn the title *Mystery* Sonatas from Biber's dedication to his employer, Archbishop Maximilian Gandolph von Khuenburgh of Salzburg, to whom he "consecrated the whole to the honor of the XV Sacred Mysteries which you promote so strongly."

Further supporting the "mystery" designation is the fact that each multi-movement work is accompanied by an engraving of an event from the 15 mysteries of the rosary—episodes from the life of Mary and Christ that Biber took from a liturgical book and pasted into the manuscript. The first five sonatas celebrate the joyous events in Mary's life: the Annunciation, the Visitation, the Nativity, the Presentation of the Infant Jesus in the Temple, and the 12-Year-Old Jesus in the Temple. The next five recount sorrowful events: the Agony in the Garden, the Scourging, the Crown of Thorns, Jesus Carries the Cross, and the Crucifixion. These are in turn followed by five miraculous events: the Resurrection, the Ascension, Pentecost, the Assumption of the Virgin, and the Beatification of the Virgin. A sixteenth work, a passacaglia with 65 variations for unaccompanied violin, to which is attached an engraving of "the Guardian Angel," stands apart from the rest, but nonetheless provides a fitting conclusion.

A number of mysteries are associated with Biber's *Mystery* Sonatas. We do not know when the collection was composed and compiled, or for what purpose. Was it intended as a private offering for the archbishop? Would it have been performed in church during October, the "rosary month," which the archbishop seems to have celebrated with particular enthusiasm? Was it composed for use at the confraternity that the archbishop founded in the name of the rosary and the Virgin Mary, one of many such confraternities emphasizing Marian piety in early modern Europe?

Finally, scholars have speculated about the precise relationship between the sonatas, the engravings, and the events they depict. Are the *Mystery* Sonatas strictly programmatic works that were composed specifically to represent the sacred episode in some literal sense, or is the correspondence one of overall mood? This question is particularly critical when we consider the most "mysterious" aspect of the sonatas: the unconventional tuning systems, or *scordature*, used in all but the first and last sonatas and given to the violinist as a diagram at the beginning of each sonata. These create dramatically different sonorities because the changes in tension necessarily alter the timbre and resonance. The retunings also allow violinists to play special double and triple stops (two and three notes at a time) that would not otherwise be possible.

The Crucifixion (Sonata No. 10) is one of the best known of the *Mystery* Sonatas. The G-minor Sonata consists of two movements: a Praeludium (in binary form) and an instrumental air (also in binary form) with five variations. The top string of the violin is tuned down a step, resulting in a tuning (top down) of D, A, D, G, rather than the normal E, A, D, G; the fourths and fifths are thus particularly resonant. In the original score (as shown in the facsimile) Biber wrote the top line a step higher, enabling the violinist to use regular fingerings without having to transpose. In the edition given here, however, the sonata is notated as it actually sounds.

The G-minor key, with its chromatic inflections, sets a somber tone appropriate for the crucifixion. Some scholars have proposed that the chords in the repeated triplets of the Praeludium refer to the hammering of the nails or to Christ's scourging, an effect that can be heightened by the performer. The lyrical instrumental air that follows, however, is not particularly mournful. Instead, the five variations of the melody become increasingly virtuosic. A brief respite in the expressive third variation, marked Adagio, sets the stage for the final two variations, the fourth with its constant sixteenth notes, and the final one with its frenetic rhythms and *stile concitato*. The latter has been associated by some commentators with the earthquake that took place during the crucifixion as reported in Matthew 27:51.

While some may interpret details of this piece as depicting the crucifixion, there is good evidence that this may not have been Biber's intent. Another copy of this sonata, wrongly attributed to the composer Johann Heinrich Schmelzer, survives in Vienna. This version also contains programmatic titles, but they have nothing to do with Christ or his crucifixion; they refer to the Turkish siege of Vienna in 1683. Since Schmelzer died before the siege, the existence of this manuscript does not challenge the attribution to Biber. It is, however, an important reminder that many of the elements that supposedly link the sonatas to the rosary mysteries may be suggestive rather than genuinely programmatic.

GEORGE FRIDERIC HANDEL (1685–1759)

Rinaldo, HWV 7a: Act 1, scenes 6, 7, and 9
Opera, 1711

Scena VI

Recitativo

12. Duetto

Scena VII

Recitativo

Rinaldo and Armida draw their swords and prepare to attack each other. In the meantine, a rock rises from underground full of dreadful monsters and, covering Armida and Almirena, carries them away, leaving in their place two hideous Furies, who, after they have mocked Rinaldo, sink and disappear.

13. Prelude

fine   *dal segno* 𝄋

14. Aria

Scena IX

Rinaldo solo

Recitativo

RINALDO

Di spe- ran- za un bel rag- gio ri- tor- ni a ri- schia- rar l'al- ma smar- ri- ta; sì, a- do- ra- ta mia

Continuo
(Violoncello,
Cembalo)

5

vi- ta! cor- ro ve- lo- ce ad op- pu- gnar gl'in- gan- ni; A- mor, sol per pie- tà, dam- mi i tuoi van- ni!

17. Aria

Allegro

Violino solo

Fagotto solo

Oboe I

Oboe II

Violino I
ripieno

Violino II
ripieno

Viola

RINALDO

Bassi
(Violoncello,
Fagotto, Cembalo)

SCENE 6

ALMIRENA

Adorato mio sposo,
vieni a bear quest'alma!

My adored spouse,
Come bless my soul!

RINALDO

Al suon di quel bel labbro
corron festosi a te gli affetti miei,
e quella fiamma illustre,
ch'in me vie più s'accende,
da' tuoi bei lumi, o cara,
prende il gran fuoco ad avamparmi
    il core.

At the sound of your beautiful lips
my affections run joyfully to you,
and that bright flame
that burns in me ever more
from your beautiful eyes, my dearest,
flares up and consumes my heart with its hot fire.

ALMIRENA

Bella stella d'amore
nelle pupille tue folgora il lume.

The beautiful star of love
flashes a light in your eyes.

RINALDO

Per te sola, o mio nume,
in dovuto olocausto,
ardon le faci mie, fuman gl'incensi
di fervidi sospiri.

For you alone, oh my goddess,
in sacrificial duty
my torches burn, and the incense smolders
from my ardent sighs.

ALMIRENA

Tu solo a' miei martiri
porgi placida calma.

You alone to my suffering
bring a peaceful calm.

RINALDO

Per te vive il mio cor, e strugge l'alma.

For you my heart lives, and my soul yearns.

NO. 12 DUET

ALMIRENA

Scherzano sul tuo volto
le grazie vezzosette
a mille a mille.

Charming graces
frolic on your face
by the thousands.

RINALDO

Ridono sul tuo labbro	*Childlike cupids*
i pargoletti amori	*laugh on your lips*
a mille a mille.	*by the thousands.*

ALMIRENA AND RINALDO

Nel bel foco di quel guardo	*In the beautiful fire of that glance*
Amor giunge al forte dardo	*Love arrives with his powerful arrow,*
care faville.	*treasured sparks.*

SCENE 7

ARMIDA

Al valor del mio brando	*To the strength of my sword*
cedi la nobil preda.	*surrender this noble prize.*

ALMIRENA

Oh Dei, che fia?	*Oh gods, what is this?*

RINALDO

Non cederò Almirena	*I will not give up Almirena,*
se col fulmine in mano	*even if Jove himself were to ask for her,*
la chiedesse il tonante.	*with a thunderbolt in his hand.*

ARMIDA

Tanto ardisci, arrogante?	*So daring, arrogant one?*

(NO. 13 PRELUDE)
NO. 14 ARIA

RINALDO

Cara sposa, amante cara,	*Dear bride, dearest lover,*
dove sei?	*where are you?*
Deh, ritorna a pianti miei!	*Ah, return to my tears!*
Del vostro Erebo sull'ara,	*On your infernal altar,*
colla face del mio sdegno	*with the fire of my wrath,*
io vi sfido, o spirti rei!	*I defy you, oh evil spirits.*

SCENE 9

RINALDO

Di speranza un bel raggio	*Would that a ray of returning hope*
ritorni a rischiarar l'alma smarrita;	*returned to console my bewildered soul,*
sì, adorata mia vita!	*yes, adored one, my life!*
Corro veloce ad oppugnar gl'inganni.	*I run quickly to uncover the deceptions.*
Amor sol, per pietà, dammi i tuo vanni!	*Love, have pity, give me your wings!*

NO. 17 ARIA

Venti, turbini, prestate	*Winds, whirlwinds, lend*
le vostre ali a questo piè.	*your wings to my feet.*
Cieli, Numi, il braccio armate	*Heavens, gods, strengthen my arm*
contro chi pena mi diè!	*against those who have given me sorrow.*

On February 24, 1711, Handel's *Rinaldo* was premiered in London at the Queen's (later King's) Theatre. Based on Tasso's *Gerusalemme liberata*, *Rinaldo*, like Lully's *Armide* (see Anthology 13), revolves around the sorceress Armida and the knight Rinaldo. The libretto by Giacomo Rossi, however, follows the Italian conventions of *opera seria* in its musico-dramatic organization in that it is primarily a series of da capo arias and recitatives, with occasional duets, such as the one included here.

Critics have credited some of the success of *Rinaldo* to the remarkable visual effects—thunder, lightning, and the rumored use of live birds, not to mention Armida's chariot, driven by two fire-breathing dragons, and the equally spectacular vocal fireworks she delivers. But the quality of the music is extraordinary throughout, despite the fact that Handel borrowed some of it from previously written compositions. No doubt the singing of the title role by Nicolini (Nicolo Grimaldi), the first castrato to take London by storm, was also a factor.

The excerpts included here from Act 1 provide a vivid sense of how action is depicted in Handel's operas, despite the relative stasis of the da capo aria. In scene 6, Rinaldo sings a duet with his beloved Almirena (albeit a bit prematurely, since her father has agreed to let them marry only after Rinaldo has taken the city of Jerusalem). In scene 7, Armida, enlisted to thwart the plans of the Christians, abducts Almirena during a brief sinfonia, leaving a melancholy Rinaldo to sing the moving aria "Cara sposa." The act ends with Rinaldo's rousing "Venti, turbini" (scene 9), in which he asks the winds to help him punish his enemies.

The opening ritornello of No. 12 (scene 6), in which the violins and oboes weave their voices together in a contrapuntal conversation in A major, provides a jovial introduction to the duet "Scherzano sul tuo volto." Although the two lovers each begin with a different couplet, Handel combines their voices in every possible way. Rinaldo imitates Almirena's line a fourth lower (mm. 12–13), and the two go on to exchange a florid melodic line (mm. 14–17), join in parallel thirds (mm. 18–19), and sing to each other in a breathless, hocket-like fashion (mm. 22–23). The contrasting **B** section (beginning at m. 32), marked poco Adagio, in triple meter and the relative minor key (C♯), is reserved for more-tender expressions of love, heightened by suspensions and hemiola rhythms in the final measures. This is followed, in performance, by a return to the playful **A** section, this time ornamented.

The furious passagework and trumpetlike repeated notes in the oboes and strings in the brief A-minor prelude near the beginning of scene 7 (No. 13) provide an apt sonic representation of the battle between Armida and Rinaldo and the appearance of the monsters that abduct Almirena. After this chaotic interlude, the introspective pathos of Rinaldo's "Cara sposa" (No. 14) is all the more moving. The long ritornello that opens the aria slows down the listener's sense of time. The violins imitate one another with a yearning line replete with poignant chromatic intrusions and sigh motives. The magical effect is enhanced by the use of *bassetto*, that is, silencing the continuo and placing it in a higher voice, as the viola plays this supportive role with its statement of a chromatic ascending line (mm. 4–7). (See Anthology 15 for another example of *bassetto*.) When Rinaldo enters in measure 12 with a simple B sustained for a full four beats, his voice seems to be floating on air, suspended in time and space until the entrance of the continuo in measure 26. Indeed, his acute sense of loss recalls that of Monteverdi's Orpheus in "Tu se' morta" (see Anthology 4).

A mere two scenes later Rinaldo regains his virility in the aria "Venti, turbini" (No. 19). For this virtuosic tour de force, Handel borrowed a violin solo from his cantata *Apollo e Dafne*, HWV 122 (Apollo and Daphne), written during his youthful Italian sojourn, depicting the sun god's frenzied pursuit of the chaste nymph. Rinaldo more than proves his heroic mettle in this aria. The entrance of the voice in measure 18 with a stunning melismatic passage brings the violins to a halt: they, like the winds that Rinaldo seeks to harness, must yield to the knight's persuasive voice. After the brief, somewhat calmer **B** section, the da capo would have provided an opportunity for Nicolini to ornament the **A** section, thus allowing the famous castrato to display even more of his vocal prowess.

Saul, HWV 53: Act 1, scene 3
Oratorio, 1738/39

22. Chorus

Tutti senza Violone

might - y King!   Wel - come all   who   Con - quest bring!

might - y King!   Wel - come all   who   Con - quest bring!

might - y King!   Wel - come all   who   Con - quest bring!

tasto solo e l'ottava colla man destra

15

30

Da - vid his Ten Thou - sands slew; Ten

Da - vid his Ten Thou - sands slew; Ten

Da - vid his Ten Thou - sands-slew; Ten

Tutti senza Violone

23. Accompagnato

24. Chorus

25. Accompagnato

26. Air

22. CHORUS

ISRAELITES

Welcome, welcome might king!
Welcome all who conquest bring!
Welcome David, warlike boy,
Author of our present joy!
Saul, who hast thy thousands slain,
Welcome to thy friends again!
David his ten thousands slew,
Ten thousand praises are his due!

23. ACCOMPAGNATO

SAUL

What do I hear? Am I then sunk so low,
To have this upstart boy preferr'd before me?

24. CHORUS

ISRAELITES

David his ten thousands slew, etc.

25. ACCOMPAGNATO

SAUL

To him ten thousands!
And to me but thousands?
What can they give him more?
Except the kingdom?

26. AIR

With rage I shall burst his praises to hear!
Oh! how I both hate the stripling, and fear!
What mortal a rival in glory can bear?

George Frideric Handel must have had something novel in mind when he composed *Saul* (1739), one of a number of his oratorios based on episodes from the Old Testament. His librettist Charles Jennens complained in a letter penned in 1738 that "Mr. Handel's head is more full of maggots than ever." One of these maggots, according to Jennens, was the very odd instrument he saw in Handel's rooms—a carillon (which today would be called a glockenspiel). This was one of several instruments inspired by accounts of music in ancient Israel that Handel planned to use in *Saul.* Described by Jennens as "a set of hammers on anvils" that was played with keys like those on a harpsichord, the carillon was intended by Handel to "make poor Saul stark mad."

The story of Saul's descent into madness over his jealousy of the young David's military triumphs provided Handel with a compelling tragic hero, and an opportunity to explore human drama on both intimate and grand scales. This, in fact, was the hallmark of Handel's English oratorios. On the one hand, as in his operas, Handel represented the private sorrows and joys of his principal characters through solo arias and duets. In this work, for example, we not only watch Saul's mental deterioration, but also witness the effect of the father's madness on his son Jonathan, who is torn between his filial duty and his love for David. On the other hand, the Israelites are also a central character in *Saul.* By incorporating the brilliant style of choral writing that English audiences knew from coronation anthems and other celebratory works, Handel introduced into the oratorio a mode of public expression that conjured up a host of familiar patriotic and religious sentiments.

Both private and public emotions are on display in Act 1, scene 3, when the carillon has its intended maddening effect on Saul. He and David have just returned triumphant from the Israelites' victory over the Philistines, in which David slew Goliath. Although Saul initially treated David warmly, even offering him his elder daughter's hand in marriage, much of the oratorio revolves around Saul's jealousy of the future king of Israel. In this scene, both David and Saul are welcomed in dance and song by a chorus of Israelites, accompanied by unison violins, continuo, and the sprightly melody of the carillon, whose ritornelli set off each line of the chorus's homophonic hymn of praise. The women begin, appropriately, by praising Saul, the mighty king. Their mistake is to heap even more praise upon David, the "author" of their present joy, whom they thoughtlessly credit with slaying 10,000 of the enemy (and thus meriting 10,000 praises) as opposed to the mere one or two thousand killed by Saul. Their error is compounded by the choral interjections at the end of the final strophe (mm. 37–44), reinforcing the phrase "ten thousands."

Saul interrupts the chorus with the first line of the ensuing accompanied recitative (No. 23). His cry "What do I hear?" calls attention to the fact that it is not only the praise of the Israelites that so enrages the king, but also the insistent sound of the carillon and female voices that begin the chorus, which, heard through Saul's ears, is more cloying than sweet. Saul's description of his sinking "so low" is manifest in the wrenching of the tonality flatward as the voice, starting on the upper C, begins a stepwise descent, which the continuo extends, ultimately landing on the low D♭ (mm. 3–4). Although

Jennens's libretto called for Saul's recitative to continue uninterrupted, Handel interjects yet another repetition of the joyful final strophe of the chorus (No. 24). If Saul was upset by the gentle praise of the women, this additional outburst is surely that much more painful, since Handel increases the sonic impact, calling for a full chorus, strings, trumpets, trombones, oboes, and timpani, in addition to the maddening carillon. Indeed, one might wonder if the enhanced orchestration is "real"—that is, part of the actual celebration—or a figment of Saul's tortured imagination.

Saul's paranoia is revealed in the remainder of the recitative (No. 25), as he, for the first time, sees David as a threat to his own power. ("What can they give him more? Except the kingdom?"). When the melancholic king vents his explosive anger in the aria "With rage shall I burst," he literally bursts in without waiting for the usual opening ritornello (No. 26). Handel underscores Saul's single-minded fury with a unison orchestral accompaniment spread across several octaves. This is followed by a sequential *stile concitato* passage, in which repeated sixteenth notes in the second violins and violas accompany the first violins' driving offbeat figure with a persistent octave drop. Although Saul himself sings in mostly longer note values, the orchestral ritornello vividly depicts the chaotic state of his psyche. Moreover, all of this is accomplished in a single stanza. Unlike the extended depiction of the grieving hero's resolve in Handel's *Rinaldo* (see Anthology 23), Saul's rage aria is not a da capo aria.

Although *Saul* is based on a biblical story, the debt of the oratorio to English theatrical traditions is apparent in the last act, when the king breaks Jewish law and consults the Witch of Endor, who conjures up the ghost of the prophet Samuel. In a stunning passage of accompanied recitative featuring trombones, Samuel foresees the destruction of Saul and the passing of the kingdom to David. After mourning the deaths of Saul and Jonathan, the Israelites reconcile themselves to their losses and declare their righteousness in battle, a message that no doubt stirred British patriotic fervor.

St. John Passion, BWV 245: Part 2, Nos. 27–32
Passion, 1724

27. Recitative

27^b. Chorus

28. Choral

Soprano / Flauto traverso I, II / Oboe I, II / Violino I: Er nahm al - les wohl in acht in der letz-ten Stun - de, sei - ne Mut-ter

Alto / Violino II: Er nahm al - les wohl in acht in der letz-ten Stun - de, sei - ne Mut-ter

Tenore / Viola: Er nahm al - les wohl in acht in der letz-ten Stun - de, sei - ne Mut-ter

Basso: Er nahm al - les wohl in acht in der letz-ten Stun - de, sei - ne Mut-ter

Continuo: col Bassono grosso

6

noch be - dacht, setzt ihr ein' Vor - mun - de. O Mensch, ma - che Rich - tig - keit, Gott und Men-schen

noch be - dacht, setzt ihr ein' Vor - mun - de. O Mensch, ma - che Rich - tig - keit, Gott und Men-schen

noch be - dacht, setzt ihr ein' Vor - mun - de. O Mensch, ma - che Rich - tig - keit, Gott und Men-schen

noch be - dacht, setzt ihr ein' Vor - mun - de. O Mensch, ma - che Rich - tig - keit, Gott und Men-schen

12

lie - be, stirb dar - auf ohn al - les Leid, und dich nicht be - trü - be!

lie - be, stirb dar - auf ohn al - les Leid, und dich nicht be - trü - be!

lie - be, stirb dar - auf ohn al - les Leid, und dich nicht be - trü - be!

lie - be, stirb dar - auf ohn al - les Leid, und dich nicht be - trü - be!

29. Recitative

Und von Stund an nahm sie der Jün-ger zu sich. Dar-nach, als Je-sus

senza Bassono grosso

wuß-te, daß schon al-les voll-bracht war, daß die Schrift er-fül-let wür-de, spricht er: Da

Mich dür-stet!

stund ein Ge-fä-ße voll Es-sigs. Sie fül-le-ten a-ber ei-nen Schwamm mit

Es-sig und leg-ten ihn um ei-nen I-so-pen, und hiel-ten es ihm dar zum Mun-de. Da nun

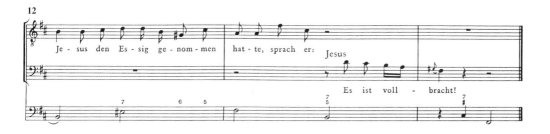

Je-sus den Es-sig ge-nom-men hat-te, sprach er:

Es ist voll-bracht!

30. Aria

31. Recitative

32. Aria

du das Haupt ____ und sprichst still-schwei-gend: ja, still-schwei-gend, still - schwei-gend: ja; doch nei-gest du das

Haupt und sprichst still - schwei - gend: ja.

27A.

EVANGELIST

Die Kriegsknechte aber, da sie Jesum gekreuziget hatten, nahmen seine Kleider und machten vier Teile, einem jeglichen Kriegesknechte sein Teil, dazu auch den Rock. Der Rock aber war ungenähet, von oben an gewürket durch und durch. Da sprachen sie untereinander:	*The soldiers, however, that had crucified Christ, took his clothing and made four parts, one part for each soldier, the same with his robe. The robe, however, had no seam, being woven through and through. They then exclaimed to one another:*

27B.

CHORUS

Lasset uns den nich zerteilen, sondern darum losen, wes er sein soll.	*Let's not divide this, rather let's toss for it, to see whose it will be.*

27C.

EVANGELIST

Auf dass erfüllet würde die Schrift, die da saget: "Sie haben meine Kleider unter sich geteilet und haben über meinen Rock das Los geworfen." Solches taten die Kriegesknechte. Es stund aber bei dem Kreuze Jesu seine Mutter und seiner Mutter Schwester, Maria, Kleophas Weib, und Maria Magdalena. Da nun Jesus seine Mutter sahe und den Jünger dabei stehen, den er lieb hatte, spricht er zu seiner Mutter:	*So that the Scripture might be fulfilled, which says: "They divided my clothing among themselves and have cast lots for my robe," these things were done by the soldiers. However, there stood by the cross of Jesus his mother and his mother's sister, Mary, Cleophas's wife, and Mary Magdalene. Now when Jesus beheld his mother and the disciple whom he loved standing by her, He said to his mother:*

JESUS

Weib, siehe, das ist dein Sohn!	*Woman, see, this is your son!*

EVANGELIST

Darnach spricht er zu dem Jünger:	*Afterwards He said to the disciple:*

JESUS

Siehe, das ist deine Mutter!	*Behold, this is your mother!*

28. CHORALE

Er nahm alles wohl in acht in der letzten Stunde, seine Mutter noch bedacht, setzt ihr ein' Vormunde. O Mensch, mache Richtigkeit, Gott und Menschen liebe, stirb darauf ohn alles Leid, und dich nicht betrübe!	*He took care of all things in the last hour, still thinking of his mother, He gave her a guardian. O mankind, make things right, love God and humanity, die afterwards without sorrow, and be without affliction.*

29.

EVANGELIST

Und von Stund an nahm sie der Jünger zu sich. Darnach, als Jesus wusste,	*And from that hour the disciple took her to his own. After this, since Jesus knew that everything*

dass schon alles vollbracht war, dass die
Schrift erfüllet würde, spricht er:

had already been accomplished, so that the
Scripture would be fulfilled, He said:

JESUS

Mich dürstet!

I thirst!

EVANGELIST

Da stund ein Gefässe voll Essigs.
Sie fülleten aber einen Schwamm
mit Essig und legten ihn um einen
Isopen, und hielten es ihm dar zum
Munde. Da nun Jesus den Essig
genommen hatte, sprach er:

There stood there a vessel full of vinegar. They
filled a spoon with the vinegar and placed it on a
hyssop branch, and held it on his mouth. Now
when Jesus had taken the vinegar, He said:

JESUS

Es ist vollbracht!

It is accomplished!

30. ARIA

Es ist vollbracht!
O Trost vor die gekränkten Seelen!
Die Trauernacht,
lässt nun die letzte Stunde zählen.
Der Held aus Juda siegt mit Macht,
und schliesst den Kampf.
Es ist vollbracht!

It is accomplished!
O comfort for the ailing soul!
The night of sorrow
now measures out its last hour.
The hero of Judah conquers with might
and concludes the battle.
It is accomplished!

31.

EVANGELIST

Und neiget das Haupt und verschied.

And bowed his head and expired.

32. ARIA AND CHORUS

Mein teurer Heiland, lass dich fragen,
da du nunmehr ans Kreuz geschlagen
und selbst gesagt: Es ist vollbracht,
bin ich vom Sterben frei gemacht?
Kann ich durch deine Pein und Sterben
Das Himmelreich ererben?
Ist aller Welt Erlösung da?
Du kannst vor Schmerzen zwar
  nichts sagen;

My precious Savior, let me ask you,
now that you have been nailed to the cross
and said to yourself: It is accomplished,
Am I free from death?
Can I, through your pain and death,
inherit the kingdom of heaven?
Is the whole world now redeemed?
You can say almost nothing out of pain;

doch neigest du das Haupt	*yet you bow your head*
und sprichst stillschweigend: ja.	*and say silently: yes.*

CHORALE

Jesu, der du warest tot	*Jesus, you who were dead*
lebest nun ohn Ende,	*now live without end*
in der letzten Todesnot,	*in the final death pangs,*
nirgend mich hinwende	*I will turn nowhere else*
als zu dir, der mich versühnt,	*but to you, who has absolved me,*
o du lieber Herre!	*O beloved Lord!*
Gib mir nur, was du verdient,	*Give me only what I merit,*
mehr ich nicht begehre!	*more I do not desire!*

On April 7, 1724, worshippers attending the Good Friday service at St. Thomas's Church in Leipzig heard the first performance of the *St. John Passion* by the 39-year-old Johann Sebastian Bach, who had begun his employment as cantor of the churches of St. Thomas and St. Nicholas the year before. The recitation of the Passion of Christ had long been an integral part of Holy Week worship in Germany, and sung sacred dramas called *historiae*, including those by Heinrich Schütz, were the predecessors of the eighteenth-century Passion settings by Bach, Handel, Telemann, and their contemporaries.

Although Passions are often considered a type of oratorio, they have a number of distinctive features. The subject matter is always the same: they focus on the events leading up to and including the crucifixion of Jesus, although the details differ depending upon which Gospel (Matthew, Mark, Luke, or John) serves as the source of the story. What makes Passions so compelling is that they do not merely provide a simple dramatic representation of the tale, as one finds in an opera or in many oratorios. Rather, a narrator called the Evangelist serves as mediator and tells the story from his point of view. Thus, several layers of commentary and contemplation enrich the Gospel text as the audience considers anew the trial and crucifixion of Jesus.

The Evangelist and the other protagonists—Jesus, Peter, and Pontius Pilate—sing in recitative. The chorus, too, plays an important role in the drama, at times impersonating the crowds of Romans and Jews who call for Jesus's crucifixion. (In the past, the recitation of the Passion often precipitated violence against Jews.) Arias and choruses featuring newly composed poetic texts offer congregants guidance in interpreting these events. The solo singers in these numbers do not play specific characters, but rather reflect on their faith and the meaning of Christ's crucifixion for the modern Lutheran believer. The chorales, sung by the chorus but familiar to the entire congregation, embody the community response.

These various layers are apparent in the climactic section of Part 2 of the *St. John Passion*. In the chorus (No. 27b), Bach's intentionally banal mode of expression heightens the listener's sense that the crowds hostile to Jesus are incapable of the introspection required of true believers. The repeated eighth notes are followed by a syncopated pattern that is imitated with mechanical precision from bass to soprano, accompanied by motoric sixteenth notes that keep the crowd riled up in an almost senseless frenzy. The Evangelist then describes the scene at the cross with the three Marys and the drinking of vinegar, punctuated by a chorale (No. 28) and brief interjections by Jesus. Bach does not portray Christ's suffering directly; we only hear his final words, "Es ist vollbracht" (It is accomplished), sung to a descending scale from D to F♯.

In the subsequent alto aria (No. 30), a meditation on the death of Christ, the solo viola da gamba plays an ornamented version of Jesus's final phrase in B minor. With its mellow and introspective timbre, dotted rhythms, and French-style ornamentation, the viol makes an intimate duet partner for the alto voice. After a modulation to D major, the upper strings join in a vigorous display of *stile concitato*. By interjecting the notion of victory and battle, Bach underscores an important point in the Gospel of St. John: that the death of Christ is a victory for humankind. It is only after this aria that the Evangelist announces Christ's passing with great simplicity (No. 31).

In the D-major bass aria (No. 32), Bach puts sorrow behind and explores the meaning of Christ's death and the phrase "es ist vollbracht." The melodic design, whereby the continuo line repeatedly ascends to the upper D by skip and half step, and the gentle $\frac{12}{8}$ meter vividly depict the newly unencumbered soul yearning for redemption; here the brighter, more modern cello playing the continuo line replaces the mellow viola da gamba of the previous aria, linked to the music of the past. The accompanying chorale expresses the tenets of faith in confident $\frac{4}{4}$ time, providing an anchor for the increasingly exuberant bass. By this point, listeners have learned to assimilate the knowledge of Christ's death into their belief in redemption and the life to come.

A year after the 1724 performance, Bach repeated the *St. John Passion* with a number of revisions, to which he added further changes in 1739. The work's final performance during Bach's lifetime in 1749 undid many of those revisions, but required a larger group of performers. This creates a quandary for modern performers. Do we try to re-create one of the known performances, or should we take into account Bach's revisions and produce a version that may be closer to his preferences later in life, but never heard by eighteenth-century listeners? Modern audiences must also grapple with the troubling anti-Judaic messages that are particularly evident in the trial scenes. It is a testament to Bach's genius that the *St. John Passion* all but transcends such questions and criticisms and has nonetheless become a universally acknowledged masterpiece of religious expression, albeit one that inevitably stimulates discussion.

JOHANN SEBASTIAN BACH (1685–1750)

The Art of Fugue, BWV 1080: Contrapuncti 1 and 7
Fugues, 1740s

Contrapunctus 1

Contrapunctus 7 a 4 per Augmentationem et Diminutionem

When Johann Sebastian Bach died on July 28, 1750, he had not yet finished revising *The Art of Fugue* for publication. Consisting of 16 fugues (one incomplete) and 4 canons based on a single theme and systematically exploring virtually every contrapuntal device, this work has a special place in Bach's oeuvre. We know from the autograph score that Bach had completed the first 14 fugues and 2 canons in the early 1740s. Yet the fact that he began revising, reordering, and adding to the work in the years just prior to his death has led scholars to regard it as a kind of musical testament. As in the Mass in B Minor of 1748–49, which ranged broadly from the *stile antico* to the most progressive "modern style," in *The Art of Fugue* the aging composer pushed beyond conventional boundaries to create another colossal work that revealed the depth and breadth of his skill.

There are still mysteries about how Bach intended these fugues and canons to be ordered and performed. While the autograph manuscript presents them in conventional keyboard score, with the contrapuntal voices distributed between the right and left hands, the printed version—the preparation of which had begun during Bach's lifetime—is not only ordered differently but is also presented in open score, meaning that each part is given its own staff, a practice that was common in the late seventeenth century but somewhat antiquated by Bach's time.

Bach's decision not to specify keyboard or any other instrumentation has also shaped the reception of *The Art of Fugue*. Was this compendium of contrapuntal techniques conceived as an abstraction, an idealized working out of musical problems that somehow transcended the need for an actual performance and performer? This view accorded with the desire of many nineteenth-century historians to see Bach's artistry as unfettered by commercial or practical considerations. Others have interpreted *The Art of Fugue* as a kind of treatise that codifies Bach's art in music rather than words. His genius is particularly evident in Contrapuncti 12 and 13, which are mirror fugues: each can be played both in its normal form and inverted to create a second fugue that is a reflection of the first.

Contrapunctus 1 is, on the surface, among the simplest and most straightforward of Bach's fugues. It lays out the theme without relying so heavily on the fugal techniques that figure prominently in the rest of the collection. These include stretto (one voice of the fugue enters with the theme before another voice has finished its statement), diminution (the theme is given in shorter note values), augmentation (the theme is given in longer note values), and inversion (the fugue subject's melodic motion is inverted, sometimes strictly and other times with adjustments that preserve the key). In the opening exposition section, the four voices enter at regular four-measure intervals. The subject in the alto is given a tonal answer in the soprano (m. 5); that is, it imitates the subject a fifth higher, albeit with alterations that preserve the D-minor tonality. (Thus, it begins with a rising fourth, from A to D, rather than a fifth.) We see the same relationship between the subject in the bass (m. 9) and its answer in the tenor (m. 13).

In measure 16, after the exposition is completed—that is, after each voice has presented the fugue theme in its entirety—we embark upon an episode, a free section in which the fugue subject is presented only partially. Bach plays a bit of a game with the listener in the next section (usually termed the counterexposition) as the voices again enter with the subject, this time in a different order and with variations. In measure 29, the soprano voice presents the opening of the subject in the dominant key. Before it is finished, however, the bass jumps in with a stretto version of the theme, this time designed to move toward the subdominant (m. 32). After an increasingly free treatment of the material, the subject reappears several times: in the tenor (m. 40), soprano (m. 49), and finally in its original form in the bass (m. 56).

The dominant pedal in the bass beginning in measure 63 signals to the listener that the end of the fugue is not far away. This leads to the most dramatic moment: the sudden halt in measure 70 on a diminished seventh chord (vii^7/i), created when the upper B♭ abruptly drops to a C♯ and the E is added in the tenor voice, sounding against the sustained B♭ in the bass and the G in the alto voice. Only after three full beats of rest does Bach trade one unstable sonority for another—landing on a second-inversion tonic chord on beat 2 of measure 71. A sense of normalcy returns in the next measure with another diminished seventh (vii^7/V) that prepares a return to the tonic. In Bach's manuscript the fugue ends with the tonic chord in measure 74. Later he added the final four measures over a tonic pedal, in which the soprano ascends into the upper register while the alto descends to low G, thus grounding the listener in the tonic key in a manner that amply compensates for the bold excursions in the proceeding measures.

Contrapunctus 7, which Bach titles "For Four Voices in Augmentation and Diminution," is even more of a contrapuntal tour de force. The basic theme that we heard in Contrapunctus 1 appears first in diminution (tenor, mm. 1–2), then in inversion (soprano, mm. 2–6); we find as well inversion and diminution (alto, mm. 3–5), and inversion and augmentation (bass, mm. 5–13). This is followed by a long episode in sixteenth notes, in which further transformations of the subject are interspersed. Note, for instance, the diminution and modulation beginning in the tenor in measure 17, where we hear the theme in B♭, followed by the use of diminution and inversion in the bass in measure 20. Beginning in measure 38, Bach places the theme in its simplest version prominently in the soprano's upper register. This leads in measure 42 to a statement by the soprano that is diminished, inverted, and rhythmically displaced. The coda, beginning at measure 56, becomes increasingly chromatic, building to the arrival on a tonic pedal in the penultimate measure and a final chord with a Picardy third.

A NOTE ON INSTRUMENTS AND SCORING IN *ANTHOLOGY OF MUSIC IN THE BAROQUE*

The changes in musical style and performance practices that mark the music of the Baroque era had a profound influence on scoring and on the use of instruments and the terms describing them. Before the Baroque, instructions for the use of specific instruments are relatively rare. By contrast, in the Baroque era indications for scoring are often abundant, although, particularly in the first half of the seventeenth century, they tend to be inconsistent. In some instances composers referred only to a member of a family of instruments (such as the generic "keyboard") or its range (treble or bass), rather than specifying the exact instrument to be used. Castello does not indicate which treble instrument should play his Sonata No. 2 from *Sonate concertate in stil moderno* (Anthology 7). The range is not suitable for soprano recorder, but the part could have been played on a violin or *cornetto*, a wind instrument with a clear, bright sound on which Castello excelled. For keyboard instruments, the terminology is often frustratingly vague. The word "cimbalo" in the title of Frescobaldi's *Toccate e partite d'intavolatura di cimbalo* (Anthology 6) may refer specifically to a harpsichord, but it was also often used generically to describe any keyboard instrument. Since Frescobaldi identifies himself as an organist on the title page of the volume, and served in that position at St. Peter's, there is every reason to assume that the works in the volume would have been played on the organ, though some may be more idiomatic for the harpsichord.

Further, this is a period in which technological advances in instrument construction and changes in styles and tastes placed newer instruments such as the violin alongside those already popular in the Renaissance, such as viols and recorders. Purcell, for instance, wrote trio sonatas for violin in the up-to-date Italian style as well as consorts for viols (see Chapter 8 of *Music in the Baroque*). Buxtehude scored his cantata cycle *Membra Jesu nostri* with violins, substituting viols in only one of the seven cantatas, *Ad cor: Vulnerasti cor meum* (Anthology 20); their mellow, introspective tone is often compared to the human voice and is appropriate for this contemplative cantata. Baroque composers also took advantage of some special instruments that are not usually heard in orchestras today, as in Vivaldi's Concerto for Viola d'amore and Lute, RV 540 (Anthology 15).

Finally, since the scoring for basso continuo was so flexible and variable, in most instances we can only guess which of the many plucked, bowed, keyboard, or lower-pitched brass and wind instruments might have been used in any given instance. While in the excerpt from Monteverdi's *L'Orfeo* (Anthology 4), the composer is explicit in calling for an *organo di legno* (a small organ with wooden pipes) and *chitarrone* (an Italian-style bass lute) for Orpheus's Act II lament, this degree of specificity is exceedingly rare. The majority of the works in the anthology have only the indication "basso" or "basso continuo." However, as Monteverdi's detailed instructions in the score of *L'Orfeo* indicate, in practice the numbers and types of instruments in the continuo group varied from one work to another, even changing within a single composition to heighten the expression and underscore dramatic changes.

The discussion below, by no means comprehensive, provides an overview of the principal instruments and vocal classifications used in the Baroque.

The viol family. Viols are bowed, fretted string instruments with six strings (seven in the case of some bass viols) that come in a number of sizes—typically treble, tenor, and bass (the approximate range of the modern violoncello), plus the violone (an octave below the bass viol). The whole family is often referred to as *viole da gamba* (viols played on or between the knees), to differentiate them from the violin family of instruments played on the arm (*viole da braccio*), of which only the large violoncello is played between the knees. However, the term *viola da gamba* most often denotes the bass viol. Viols were particularly prized in polyphonic music, often composed for consorts of five or six instruments. Variants of the bass viol included the division viol, a small bass viol used in England as a solo instrument, especially for highly ornamented music; and the lyra viol, a small bass viol built and tuned to facilitate playing chords with the bow.

The violin family. Violins are bowed, unfretted instruments with four strings. Like viols, they come in different sizes. The standard members of the violin family are the treble violin (known as the violin); the viola, which plays in the alto range, tuned a fifth lower than the violin; and the violoncello, in the bass range, tuned an octave below the viola. The largest of *da braccio* instruments, variously called the contrabass, double bass, or violone, usually plays an octave below the cello, but during the Baroque it was far less standardized than the other violins in terms of design, range, and number of strings, and there was also a violone that, although large, sounded at the same pitch as the cello.

French music from the seventeenth and eighteenth centuries often featured as many as three parts for different-sized violas, which, although tuned the same way, had somewhat different timbres that enriched the preferred five-part string scoring. These ensembles included the *haut-contre* or countertenor viola, the *taille* or tenor, and the *quinte* or second tenor (see Anthology 19). Other members of the violin family include the small *violino piccolo* (usually tuned a third or fourth higher than the standard violin), which Bach used in his Brandenburg Concerto No. 1; the even smaller *pochette* or pocket violin used by dancing masters; and the viola d'amore, which resembles a large viola (though often in an unusual shape). In addition to its bowed strings (usually five to seven), this "love viol" (often in an unusual shape) includes six or seven strings attached under the fingerboard that vibrate sympathetically, creating a rich, shimmering sound (see Anthology 15).

Plucked strings (non-keyboard). Baroque players had a variety of plucked stringed instruments at their disposal, many of which were used as part of the continuo group. The lute could also be used as a solo instrument or to accompany songs (see Anthology 3). Its strings, which in the Baroque typically numbered 24, were arranged in courses or pairs (except for the top two, which were single strings). Bass lutes (or archlutes), used as continuo instruments, included the theorbo and the *chitarrone*. Other popular plucked instruments included the cittern, which has a flat back and resembles a modern banjo or mandolin; and the guitar, usually flat-backed or slightly rounded. Harps of various sizes, ranging from single harps that could only play diatonic pitches to triple harps that could play the chromatic notes, were also an important element in continuo groups.

Keyboard. In the Baroque period, keyboard instruments were used both in continuo groups and as solo instruments. The harpsichord and organ were the standard keyboard instruments of the Baroque, and here again there was considerable variety in style and construction. The sound of a harpsichord was produced when strings were plucked by *plectra* (usually made of bird quills or leather). Each plectrum was held by an ingenious mechanism known as the "jack." When the key was depressed, the jack was raised and the plectrum plucked the string. Harpsichords typically had one manual (keyboard), but sometimes two or three, and could also have two or more sets of strings (registers) controlled by hand stops to vary the color and intensity of the sound. A variant of the harpsichord that was popular in England was the virginal or virginals, a small, single-manual harpsichord, often shaped in a rectangle or polygon so it could be easily moved and used in domestic settings.

Organs were wind instruments: their sound was produced by air blown through a set of pipes, the wind supply being produced by a set of bellows not unlike those found in blacksmith shops, although much larger, which were usually operated by energetic boys or young men. Organs of this period ranged from the large, impressive instruments of northern Germany (see *Music in the Baroque*, Figure 4.3), which could feature two, three, and even more manuals, a pedal board, and a wide variety of registers (sets of pipes, each controlled by a single stop), to the small, single-manual portative organs with wooden pipes, such as the *organo di legno* in *L'Orfeo*.

Finally, the clavichord was a small keyboard instrument favored by many keyboard professionals. Its sound was produced when a piece of wood, leather, or metal called the *tangent* struck a string. The sound of the clavichord is very soft and only suitable for solo playing in an intimate setting. However, it is remarkably expressive, since, unlike the harpsichord plectrum, the tangent remains in contact with the string until the key is released, allowing dynamic variation, small alterations in tone, and even the production of vibrato.

Brass and wind instruments. Wind and brass players used many of the same instruments as their counterparts in the Renaissance, though the instruments' functions expanded considerably. The trumpet, lacking the valves of the modern instrument, shifted from being primarily used for military signals to chamber and solo use, and by the eighteenth century required considerable virtuosity. The horn, associated with the hunt and the outdoors, joined the orchestra in the late Baroque, particularly for festive occasions. The trombone (the early version of which was known as the sackbut) was featured in independent brass ensembles and to accompany singers (the slide made it easy to match pitches). The tenor-ranged trombone became the standard, and was often associated with the underworld or death (see Anthology 10).

There is no real modern equivalent for the *cornetto*, a curved wooden instrument with a bright, penetrating sound produced with a mouthpiece similar to those of trumpets.

The woodwinds of the Baroque included a wide variety of recorders, flutes, and reed instruments. Of the many members of the recorder family (including sopranino, soprano, alto, tenor, bass, and contrabass), the soprano and alto remained the most popular. Most references to "flute" in Baroque scores actually mean recorder. When composers wanted the "transverse" flute, played sideways like the modern flute (but made of wood and often with a single key), they indicated this specifically with the term "flauto traverso" (see Anthology 25). The French flageolet (see Anthology 19) was a somewhat simpler version of the soprano recorder, with fewer finger holes and a bright, birdlike sound.

The Baroque oboe, which featured a conical bore and double reed, was essentially a modernized version of the Renaissance shawm. Oboes were particularly valued in Baroque orchestras for the way they blended with violins (see Anthology 19 and 23). The oboe d'amore (see Anthology 25) is slightly larger than the oboe, in the mezzo-soprano range, with a somewhat sweeter, less penetrating tone. Bassoons, double-reed instruments that played in the bass range, were also popular in the Baroque, used in ensembles and continuo groups, and occasionally as solo instruments; the larger contrabassoon sounds an octave lower.

Percussion. Although we find relatively few indications for percussion instruments in the Baroque until the eighteenth century, this does not mean they weren't used, especially in music played outdoors for festive and military occasions, or for special theatrical effects. Like trumpets, field drums would have been used for military signals, while hand drums and tambourines might accompany dancing. All sorts of percussion instruments were part of military bands and were later incorporated into orchestras. Some (likely kettle drums) might have been used in Rameau's *Platée* (Anthology 19) to represent the clap of thunder. Handel's *Saul* (Anthology 23) calls for a "carillon," referring to a glockenspiel, a percussion instrument fitted with a keyboard that caused bells or metal bars to be struck by a hammer.

Vocal casting and names. The majority of scores for vocal music in *Anthology of Music in the Baroque* follow modern practice, referring to the voice parts as soprano, alto, tenor, and bass. As with instruments, voice parts in scores from the first half of the seventeenth century use terminology from the Renaissance: thus we find *canto* or *cantus* for soprano, and *quinto* or *quintus* for an additional tenor (see Anthology 1). The terms "soprano" and "alto" refer only to vocal range and provide no indication as to whether the singer was male or female. In the seventeenth century, with the exception of music performed in convents or female orphanages (see *Music in the Baroque*, Chapter 9), boys, falsettists, and castrati invariably sang the soprano and alto parts in liturgical music, and in most paraliturgical music as well (see *Music in the Baroque*, Chapter 5). Thus, in Carissimi's *Jephte* (Anthology 11), the part of the daughter would have been sung by a male, likely a boy. Handel's oratorios, however, performed in London theaters rather than churches, featured female soloists (see Anthology 23).

The situation is more complicated in secular music; here women often, but not always, sang the upper voices. A female soprano would have sung the role of Hypsipyle in Cavalli's *Giasone* on the Venetian stage (Anthology 12), but the role would likely have been sung by a man in the Roman production of *Il novello Giasone*, since women were forbidden to sing in public in Rome. In France, where castrati were not widely accepted, female singers did appear on the stage. Rameau's *Platée* (Anthology 19), however, features an *haut-contre* (countertenor), a high male voice favored by the French, in the role of the female swamp creature.

GLOSSARY OF PERFORMANCE INDICATIONS

à 2 cordes [Fr.] On two strings.

à 3 cordes [Fr.] On three strings.

à demi [Fr.] Used synonomously with the Italian term *mezza voce* ("half voice"); also indicates a dynamic level midway between piano and forte.

à demi doux [Fr.; *mezzo piano*, It.] Moderately soft.

à demi fort [Fr.; *mezzo forte*, It.] Moderately loud.

accompagnato [It.] Accompanied; used to describe a recitative accompanied by instruments in addition to the basso continuo.

Adagio [It., "at ease"] Very slowly.

adoucissant [Fr.] Softening.

allegro [It.] Lively, merry; used to indicate a moderately fast tempo.

alto [It.; *altus*, Lat.; "high"] Generally, the second-highest voice in a four-part vocal ensemble or an instrument that plays in a middle range, lower than that of a soprano and higher than the tenor.

andante [It., "walking"] Moderately slowly.

andante allegro [It.] Somewhat livelier than *andante*.

arpégement [Fr.; arpeggio, It.] Ornament whereby the notes of the chord are played successively rather than simultaneously.

aspiration [Fr., "inhalation"] Indication to play the note short and sharply.

avec clavecin [Fr.] With the harpsichord.

basso [It.; basse, Fr.; bassus, Lat.] Bass; the lowest voice in a vocal ensemble; also the lowest instrumental part, often providing the basis for the harmony.

basso continuo, bc [It.] Instrumental bass line over which the keyboard or plucked string instruments improvise or realize the chords indicated by numbers and symbols.

bassono grosso [It.] Contrabassoon.

Bns [abbrev.] Bassoons.

BVn [abbrev.] Bass violin or cello.

canto [It.; *cantus*, Lat.] Soprano or top voice.

cembalo [It.] Harpsichord.

chitarrone [It.] Bass lute or theorbo.

chorus ad libitum, lib. [Lat.] Chorus to be added as desired.

clavecin [Fr.] Harpsichord.

col bassono grosso [It.] With the contrabassoon.

con sordino [It.] With the mute.

continuo [It.] See *basso continuo*.

contrabasso [It.] Contrabass or bass violin.

cordes [Fr.] Strings.

couplets [Fr.] Episodes in a rondeau (rondo) form.

croches égales [Fr.] Eighth notes played evenly (see *notes égales*).

da capo [It.] From the top or beginning.

dal segno [It.] Indication to repeat from the sign 𝄋.

demi doux [Fr.; *mezzo piano*, It.] Moderately softly.

dessus hautbois, DHb [Fr.] Top oboe.

dessus violin, DVn [Fr.] Top violin.

détaché [Fr.] Detached.

doux [Fr.] Soft.

en glissant [Fr., "sliding"] Indication to the violinist to play the two successive notes by sliding one finger between them.

esclamazione, escl. [It., "exclamation"] Vocal ornament in which the singer first relaxes the voice and then increases the intensity.

fagotto [It.] Bassoon.

flauto traverso, tr. [It.] (Transverse) flute.

fine [It.] End; indication to conclude the movement.

forte, f [It; fort, Fr.] Loud.

gai [Fr.] Cheerful.

gayement [Fr.] Cheerfully.

haut-contre [Fr.] Countertenor; refers to a male singer in a higher range than the tenor or an instrument in that range.

haut-contre viola, HCVn [Fr.] Countertenor viola (smaller than the tenor).

lamento [It.] Lament.

largo [It., "broad"] In a slow tempo, with dignified affect; generally slower than *andante* but not as slow as *adagio*.

lent, lentement [Fr.; lento, It.] Slow, slowly.

misura, mis. [It.] Beat.

molt' adagio [It.] Extremely slow.

mordent [from *mordere*, It. (to bite); *pincé*, Fr.] 𝆕 Three-note ornament featuring a single, quick alternation between the main note and the note below.

notes égales [Fr., "equal notes"] Indication that the eighth or sixteenth notes should be played evenly, in contrast to the unwritten French performance practice of playing a series of equal notes in a long-short pattern, called *notes inégales*.

oboe d'amore, Oboe d'am [It., "oboe of love"] Oboe in the alto range.

org. tasto solo e l'ottava [It.] Indication for organist to play only the bass line an octave higher.

org. pieno [It.] Full organ; indication that the organ should be played with the majority of stops pulled out to achieve the fullest, most brilliant sound.

organo, org. [It.] Organ.

organo di legno [It.] Organ with wooden pipes.

ossia col continuo sino al (segno) [It.] Alternatively with continuo until the sign.

parties [Fr., "parts"] Term used to describe the middle string parts (countertenor and tenor violas) in late seventeenth- and eighteenth-century French music (Anthology 19).

pianissimo, pp [It.] Very soft.

piano, p [It.] Soft.

plus lent [Fr.] More slowly.

port de voix [Fr., "carrying of the voice"] 𝅘𝅥𝅮 Appoggiatura-like ornament in which the non-chord tone, pictured with a small-sized note, is played or sung just before the main tone, executed with varying rhythms depending on the context.

praeludium (Lat.) Prelude.

Presto [It.] In a very quick tempo.

Quinto [It.; quinte, Fr.; *Quintus*, Lat., "fifth"] Name for an additional voice filling the texture, usually in alto (Anthology 1) or tenor range (Anthology 13).

QVn [Fr.] *Quinto* or second tenor viola part.

recitativo [It.; *récit*, Fr.] Recitative.

ritardando, rit [It.; *en retard*, Fr.] Slowing down.

ritornello [It.] Instrumental refrain.

rondeau [Fr.] The refrain in a rondo form, which alternates with the episodes or *couplets*.

sans clavecin [Fr.] Without harpsichord.

Sempre [It.] Always.

senza bassono grosso [It.] Without a contrabassoon (Anthology 25).

simile [It.] In a similar way.

sinfonia [It.] Symphony; movement, often introductory, to be played by instruments.

solo [It.; plural, *soli*] Indication that only the soloist or soloists play.

soprano [It.] Generally, the highest vocal or instrumental range.

spiccato [It.] Bouncing the bow lightly off the string.

tasto solo   [It.] Indication for basso continuo to play the bass line without chords.

tasto solo e l'ottava colla man destra   [It.] Indication for a keyboard player to play the bass line only, an octave higher and with the right hand.

tenore   [It.] Tenor; used in the Baroque and later to refer to the highest male voice sung with normal production (not falsetto) and the instruments that play in that range.

tous à deux cordes   [Fr.] All on two strings (of the violin).

tremolo, trem.   [It.] Vocal or instrumental embellishment consisting of a rapid reiteration of one or more notes (Anthology 7 and 14).

trill, tr, t   [*trillo*, It; *tremblement* +, Fr.] Embellishment consisting of a rapid alternation between two adjacent notes, usually beginning with the upper note; the early-seventeenth-century *trillo* (t.) featured increasingly rapid reiterations of a single note (Anthology 2).

tutti   [It.] All play.

tutti senza violone   [It.] All play except the bass violin or contrabasses.

viola d'amore   [It., "viola of love"] Instrument of the *da braccio* family the size of a large viola and with sympathetic strings.

viola da gamba, Va. da g.   [It.] Fretted bowed stringed instrument played between the legs (*da gamba*).

violino, vn   [It.] Violin.

un peu fort   [Fr.] A little louder.

un peu vite   [Fr.] A little faster.

un peu pointé   [Fr.] A bit more dotted (as opposed to equal or *égales*) (Anthology 19).

Variation   [It.] Variation.

Vif   [Fr.] Lively.

Vite   [Fr.] Fast.

Vivace   [It.] Lively.

volti   [It., "turn"] Indication to turn the page quickly.